HOLGA
THE WORLD
THROUGH A
PLASTIC
LENS

lomography

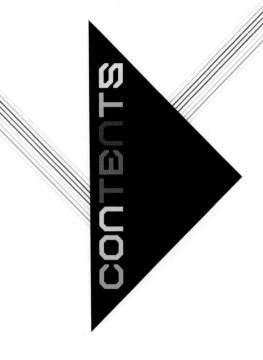

CONTENTS

Intoxicating country music, rattling carousels, candyfloss, real women with enormously short skirts and real men in enormously pointy cowboy boots. You are back in the late 1980s at a carnival in the midst of the deepest U.S. backwater. Bang, Zing, Thud! The bullets are whizzing around your ears. You've arrived at the shooting stands. And now take a good look. What's that, hiding between those plastic radios, vases and stuffed animals, the prizes on offer to the sharpest of sharp-shooting boys and girls? A Holga!

Believe it or not, the Holga (a plastic low-tech camera developed in Hong Kong in 1982) began its triumphal procession through the Western world of photography at just such carnivals in the late 1980s. At first shooting stands had another legendary Hong Kong-made cheapo camera called 'Diana' among the prizes on show (search the web for the Diana - it's worth it!). However when they went out of production a replacement was required, and the Holga was to be it. But it didn't stop there. Even college professors who teach photography like going to folk gatherings, and so it came to pass that the Holga had soon wandered from the carnivals to the photography colleges and art universities. Here people valued the camera's simplicity, its total lack of complexity, recommending it to students with the words "learn to look before you take photographs." So the Holga soon drifted from hand to hand across the full length and breadth of that vast land, becoming better known over the years. And a number of those sprogs who learned to "look" with the Holga later became world famous photographers, so the camera soon had a reputation in glossy magazine circles. Surprisingly, it took a long time for this phenomenon, this genuine 'American dream', to drift on across the herring pond to Europe. In fact, it was not until the second half of the 1990s that it did. At that time, dear friend, the freshly founded Lomographic Society International discovered the camera, began to love and cherish it, and to spread the merry message of the Holga. And now she has come into her own, with a whole book dedicated just to Holga!

The shot from the hip, the restless photographic documentation of your everyday life and as many impossible snapshots as possible taken in the most impossible positions possible in the most impossible of situations possible - that's Lomography! But, of course, if you're already a Lomographer you've known that for ages. However if you've never heard of this world wide movement then you'd better snoop around at www.lomography.com or just keep reading here anyway, and see if the Holga isn't an optimum introduction to the Lomographic world of images.

The Holga you see, dear (fledgling) Lomographer, fits seamlessly into the collection of Lomographic cameras, all of which are quite unpredictable, moody and, in their own way, ingenious. Just like the Lomo LC-A, with which the concept of Lomography was born, the Holga promises *a priori* nothing whatsoever! As ever, it's all down to you. Your mood and whim, your style and the way you look and think or don't look and don't think determine what comes out in the images. And as if that's not tricky enough, as soon as you've pressed the button to take the shot the Holga does its own thing altogether and, depending on the camera's mood, produces either the most enormous crap you've ever seen, or the most wonderful image ever to have caressed your oppressed creative soul.

"Lomography's all about not following any rules (see: the 10 golden rules of Lomography *) and yielding fully to one's own moods as well as the whims of highly idiosyncratic cameras, in order to become a truly virtuoso Lomographer. Why, though, is this book so totally bulging with the most artful of tips & tricks, awe-inspiring Lomographer profiles by Holga connoisseurs and, then, the whole lot accompanied by simply fabulous shots?" Dear friend, you answer your own query. This book is supposed to do neither more nor less than give your imagination a lift, to get you itching to get into some seriously heavy duty snapshooting for yourself. We'll do whatever it takes to find what it is that will seduce you into tasting the sweet fruits of Lomography, and that with the greatest of pleasure.

All the Holga masterpieces that you see in this book were sent in over the course of what we called the Holga Rumble, a worldwide appeal to the international Lomography community. All the tips & tricks come 100% from veteran warhorses and honourable members of the www.lomography.com community. All of the profiles in this book are genuine portraits and self-portrayals of real free-range Lomographers! And the whole excellent idea stems, ladies and gentlemen, from: Adam Scott.

Who the hell is Adam Scott (and his friend 9T)?

Adam Scott is not only a nice well brought-up young man, but also a diligent Lomographer and a professional photographer who has excellent ideas - and thankfully shares the latter with us. A simple E-mail addressed to the bigwigs at Lomography HQ turned into a trip to Vienna, a beer turned into two hundred beers, a long night into a good plan - and from there on it was all plain sailing. Rumble, 2500 - submitted Holga shots, 300 tips & tricks, innumerable profiles, text passages, layout ideas, hysterics, ritual dances ...and in the end, now this nifty little tome lies before you. This volume is the heart-blood of Holga-Lomographic passion! Anything else that Adam Scott would like to say is not only written on the next couple of pages, it's also clear to see throughout this book. With the help of his no less talented and very congenial designer friend 9T he was responsible for selecting only the very finest pieces from the veritable flood of images that came in - a nightmare of a task. Only truly taste-talented tuffguys like Adam and 9T could have mastered the task with such virtuosity. Not to mention the superhuman exertions involved in the layout - poor 9T, thanks 9T, it's a real beauty 9T! What we'd still like to say? A bumper thank you, too, to all the Lomographers around the world who have, so to speak, designed this book themselves with their photos. This is Lomography!

Adam Scott

Ninety

★ GOLDEN RULES OF LOMOGRAPHY

1 TAKE YOUR CAMERA EVERYWHERE YOU GO.
2 USE IT ANY TIME - DAY AND NIGHT.
3 LOMOGRAPHY IS NOT AN INTERFERENCE IN YOUR LIFE, BUT PART OF IT.
4 TRY THE SHOT FROM THE HIP.
5 APPROACH THE OBJECTS OF YOUR LOMOGRAPHIC DESIRE AS CLOSE AS POSSIBLE.
6 DON'T THINK (WILLIAM FIREBRACE).
7 BE FAST.
8 YOU DON'T HAVE TO KNOW BEFOREHAND WHAT YOU CAPTURED ON FILM.
9 NOR AFTERWARDS.
10 DON'T WORRY ABOUT ANY RULES.

1982	The first Holga runs off the conveyor belt in Hong Kong, originally conceived as a cheap medium format camera for the US-market and for American photography schools
1986	Cui Jian, the 'godfather of Chinese rock', storms the Chinese charts with *I Own Nothing*
Late-1980s	Production of the Diana (another cheap medium format camera) ceases and opens a market niche for the Holga in the West. The Holga first appears at carnivals in the USA, and becomes known at American photo colleges and art colleges, e.g. being offered at Maine Photographic Workshops
1992	The Lomographic Society International is founded and the 10 golden rules of Lomography are being developed
1992	Tang Dynasty release *Dreaming Back to Tang Dynasty*, the first heavy Metal album in the history of Chinese music
1998	Michael Zollner writes for the first time about the Holga in Europe, in the German *Fotomagazin*
1998	Thousands of enquiries from Europe follow; at the time the Holga could only be ordered directly in the USA
2001	The Holga is accepted as a qualifying camera in the Lomographic Sampling Games; the Lomographic Society sells the Holga online and at selected stores
2002	Fred Lebain publishes his book *Mes Vacances avec Holga*
2003	The Lomographic Society brings the Holga Starter Kit onto the market and makes the Holga world famous at last. www.lomography.com/holga

INTRODUCTION

BY ADAM SCOTT

Did you think your eyes were open? I'm afraid to say that until this very moment they have been closed. This book is here to save you from a future of digital pixels and images shared on small screens on cameras or phones. We have all become numbed with photography, there is no denying it, but a chunky camera made almost entirely of plastic has been put on this Earth to save us. It will reawaken your vision, fill you with joy and make you see beauty when you thought it had disappeared forever.

Made in Hong Kong in 1982, yet given a distinctly European name, the Holga seems more a toy likely to spray water at your face than a means to take a photo. The name Holga is a re-interpretation (possibly to make it more attractive to the European market) of the Cantonese word 'ho gwong' meaning 'very bright'. It takes 120 medium format film - preferred by professional photographers - as opposed to the conventional 35mm film that we are all familiar with. Cameras in this department tend to cost a lot of money. The Holga however, aside from the shutter spring and a couple of screws, is made entirely of plastic - including the lens! We are faced with an initial contradiction that makes the Holga positively ironic - a cheap plastic camera that takes professional quality film. The camera itself is probably worth less than the expense of a roll of film, processing and prints. However, once you have shot that roll of film and seen the results, the economic value will become secondary to its priceless beauty.

Because of its inexpensive nature, the Holga is categorized as a 'Toy Camera'. There are many discontinued 'toys' in this alternative branch of photography, but due to its worldwide popularity, the Holga is still being made. You don't need to be an expert to decide which of the two light settings, four focusing modes and two shutter speeds to choose from. It's this simplicity that gives it a 'toy' status, but to have fun with photography you will need a toy - so why not play with the Holga?

The lack of options with the Holga makes it an unpredictable and very exciting camera to use. You will find yourself asking whether a shot is in focus, or correctly exposed, or whether you remembered to wind the film forward or even take the lens cap off. More importantly, you will question whether you even care! After you use the Holga for a while - if you don't give up on it - you will become used to how it works and even adapt to how it sees, but you will never fully understand it.

It's easy to see images taken by the Holga and assume that once the camera is loaded, any shot will be magically transformed into a work of art. This isn't the case. A grey day will give you a dull shot and an ugly subject will produce an unattractive image. On occasion, you may only find merely one good shot on an entire roll or that every shot is fantastic. The real trick is to persevere with it and to decide what is the best environment for you and your Holga to get along. The Holga is a truly personal choice – you may actually like that grey day or ugly subject that NO ONE else would ever shoot. When you get that perfect Holga shot that you love it is priceless, and worth all the time and energy spent on rolls of films that weren't to your satisfaction.

Many people have different views as to what makes the Holga so special. Could it be the light leaks? Is it the vignette around the edges or soft focus near the center of the image? Perhaps it's the Holga's simple and rudimentary looks or the fact that it's so cheap that you can perform any kind of modification or personalization to it without feeling the economical impact too much. Every Holga photographer has different opinions but all have one thing in common: their love and devotion to their Holga and, in many cases, a full-blown clinical obsession. Within this book, in cooperation with the Lomographic Society International (LSI), I want to showcase the work of many people from all over the world who are united by this unique camera. You'll also see a wealth of tips and tricks that can turn anyone into a great Holga shooter.

My love affair began when I discovered the Lomographic Society International. They sold the Holga and I was intrigued by its contradiction in terms of a cheap medium format camera. As I opened the box and took the camera out I thought I had been ripped off! It was too light and cameras were not meant to be this light. I shot a roll of film while taking a walk in London and there it was, the addiction had begun. A couple of accidental double exposures showed me what the Holga was capable of doing. I had already been shooting for many years with single lens reflex cameras and was beginning to get bored of photography, but the Holga reopened my eyes and injected me with a new love. I felt as though I had discovered a new sense or a new colour.

Putting this book together was by no means a simple process, although the LSI made the challenge a lot easier to face. A simple email to Lomography ended with drunken adventures in Vienna followed by a meeting with a handful of Austrians. This book could only have been achieved with their help. Not only are they always excited to take part in new projects, but they have the resources, and members to create a truly International book with images submitted from all over the world.

The Holga is just a plastic camera. In the right hands, however, it can produce beautiful, stimulating and inspiring images that may force you to put down your digital interpolation machines and turn you on to a world of plastic photography.

A HOLGA OVERVIEW

In the Holga family there are three different medium format cameras:
The Holga 120S, 120SF and the latest 120CFN. The first two have one shutter speed, two lighting modes and four focusing positions. The 120S has a hot shoe for the flash and the 120SF has a built-in flash. The new 120CFN has a built-in flash with variable colour gels, two shutter speeds and a tripod mount.
see: www.lomography.com/holga

6x6

The Holga has two image modes. The most popular is 6X6 format that produces twelve square images on one normal 120mm film. There is something about a square image that makes it unique and interesting. Perhaps it's the fact that we are so used to rectangle images - whether in portrait or landscape - that a square Holga photo seems or becomes unconventional and attractive.

6X6 Holga images are soft around the centre and - depending on the lighting - there will be a varied amount of vignette. These traits draw the viewer to the image giving it a sense of movement. This may be one of the reasons why the square Holga shot is so popular and attractive.

OVERVIEW

6x4.5

Although 6x6 is the signature Holga format, if you are running low on cash and need more shots there is also the 6x4.5 frame mode. With 6x4.5 you will get 16 rectangular images out of one roll of film. The adaptor, a simple plastic unit that you insert in the back of the camera, converts the square image into a rectangular one. It also helps to keep the batteries in place in the Holga 120SF and the Holga 120S, and is reported to reduce light leaks from the front of the camera. This frame mode also eliminates the vignette while maintaining the softness around the centre of the image. You need to remember to turn the Holga onto its side for landscape images - as it produces rectangular, portrait images in the normal upright mode.

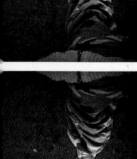

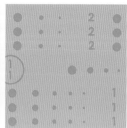
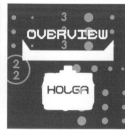

FILM TYPES

With the Holga you can use all types of 120 film. 120 film is a medium format film that is mainly used by professional photographers. Due to its larger size, you will be able to blow up an image with better results than 35mm. To find this film you will have to go to professional photographic stores and can't expect to see it at your local supermarket. Already at this early stage you need to make a little more effort than usual.

Remember, just like you and me, the Holga loves the sun! When using regular colour film, it's important to note that better results will be achieved when shooting in bright sunlight. If your subject is against the sun, the flash on the Holga can be used as a fill and will help you maintain detail and avoid a person becoming a silhouette. Unless this is what you want to achieve. The colour gels on the flash will also tint close subjects in your chosen colour while everything out of the flash range will remain in natural light. It essentially creates layers and doesn't colour the entire image like a filter. Check out the Tips and Tricks later in this book to see what else you can do with the flash.

FILM TYPES

The Holga is capable of producing stunning black & white images. You can also shoot more freely with black & white film on a cloudy day than with colour film. Black & white is fantastic for characteristic portraits and moody landscapes. The wide lens on the Holga gives a great effect when capturing a solitary object, person or building in the middle of an interesting surrounding. If you like to spend hours in a dark room with only the smell of chemicals to keep you company, then printing your own black & white Holga images is always an option.

OVERVIEW

HOLGA

FILM TYPES

To get outrageous colours, try cross processing. This consists of developing a slide film (the film your grandparents used to bore the hell out of you with their projected holiday snaps when you were a kid) as if it were a normal colour negative film. Usually, your slide film goes through a process called E-6. You'll get normal slides out of this standard procedure. However, seeing as the 'hold a slide to the light and look at it with one eye closed' days are over, ask your local lab technician (nicely) to process your slide film in C-41 (which is what you normally use for 35mm colour negative film) and see what you get out of it. By putting the slide film into the chemicals, the colours become displaced and your image explodes with brightness, saturation, and contrast. see: www.lomography.com/x

The unpredictability of results is perfect for the Holga photographer and gives the photo an even softer edge. Each film and laboratory will produce different results. If you do your own prints both digitally or in a lab you will have more control over the final result.

● ● ●

LIGHT LEAKS

OVERVIEW

HOLGA

The most unique and trademark aspect of the Holga are light leaks. The camera is so cheap that light can penetrate the Holga and produce light incidences on your negative. This can be anything from a slight red tint on the frame to a fully burnt out image with the film exposure number and designation burning onto the negative. For many, this occurrence is their favourite Holga effect. It's most likely to happen in bright sunlight. If you drop the Holga on the floor it will undoubtedly open. If you cover the back and close it quickly you may not lose all the info on the negative and might be pleasantly surprised with some cool light leaks. Light leaks also occur when you finish the film and it's slightly loose on the spool. If you want to avoid this, then buy a small changing bag from a professional photographic store and take the film out inside the changing bag. Once the film is out of the Holga you will need to unwind it and re-wind it tightly.

MULTIPLE
EXPOSURES

Most cameras have a mechanism that prevents you from taking two photos on the same bit of film. After taking a photo you are forced to wind the film forward to take another shot. 120 film, however, shows its exposure number on paper behind the film itself. A small red window on the back of the Holga allows you to see what image number you are on. This makes it possible to take as many shots on one frame as desired, well, as long as you don't completely overexpose the negative or break your trigger finger! This feature can be manipulated and used to your favour or it might accidentally ruin a single exposure photo. It's easy to forget to wind the film forward so you can decide to always wind the film after a shot or before taking another photo or try to not care and see what happens. In the right hands and with a bit of luck, multiple exposures can create complex and stunning images and also turn accidental double exposures into photographic miracles.

OVERLAPPED
EXPOSURES

This freedom of movement with the film inside the Holga can create another effect. It's possible to expose the negative and then to partially wind on the film and take another shot. This will cause the images to overlap. Essentially, one could expose the entire film like this creating a huge panoramic image of overlapped photos. In the 6x6 format the different exposures will fade into each other while the 6x4.5 will create distinct lines between the frames. It's hard to predict the outcome when using this technique and you will require a scanner to deal with longer images, as conventional labs can't cater for such long negatives.

 HOLGA OVERVIEW

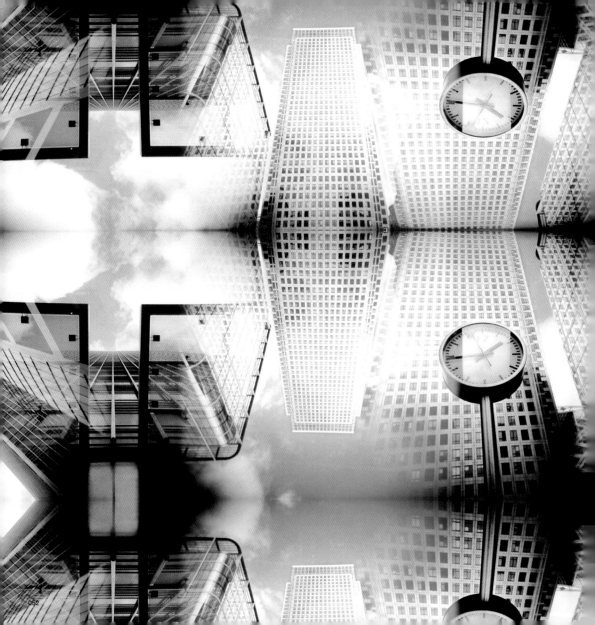

LONG EXPOSURES

The Holga 120 CFN has a Bulb 'B' setting so that the shutter will stay open for as long as you keep the release depressed. With this feature, you will be able to take long-exposure night shots or pick up the ambient light when shooting in clubs and bars. If you want a sharp image you will need to use a tripod, otherwise you can choose to go for the abstract blurs with the flash as a fill.

FILTERS OVERVIEW

If you want to enhance your image even further, check out the filter set, (see www.lomography.com/holga). They do exactly what they say on the tin. 4 colour filters with a clean hole in the middle will direct the line of vision even more to the centre of the image while giving a surround colour of your choice. The other four filters are solid; these can either create an overlay on colour film or enhance certain tones of black and white images. You'll want to use faster film when using the colour filters, as they block a considerable amount of incoming light. On a sunny day for example you will be better off with 400 ASA speed film as opposed to 100 ASA. There are also split image filters that instantly multiply the image you have just photographed which can be used to create abstract images when combined with multiple exposures.

COLOUR FLASH

The flash on the Holga 120 CFN includes built-in colour gels. This way you can tint your shots with colour or create weird portraits of people at night. Use it as a fill light with colour during the day where nearby subjects will be coloured in while maintaining the natural light in the background or enhance your double exposures with one frame of colour. The possibilities and combinations are endless.

 HOLGA OVERVIEW

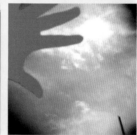

35mm

HOLGA OVERVIEW

A   B   C

One of the best modifications that can be done to the holga is turning it into a 35mm camera. Firstly, you need to tape the beginning of a roll of film to the plastic spool that goes in the left hand side of the holga (A). You need to avoid light going into the camera as 35mm film doesn't have a protective paper backing like 120 film. To do this you must tape up the film counter window of the holga on both sides (B). Finally, insert the film in the left side of the holga and secure it in place with two pieces of sponge (C). Place the spool in the right side of the holga as usual (C) and close the back. After each photo, wind the camera forward as normal and count the amount of clicks. It usually takes thirty or thirty-five clicks for each photo to avoid overlapping of the images. When you finish the roll of film you will need to go into a dark room to open the back of the holga, take out the film and rewind it manually. Once all the film is rewound you can take it to the lab for normal processing. Please pay attention to the lab technician's shocked expression when they see an image on a negative that goes over the sprockets for the first time in the lives!.

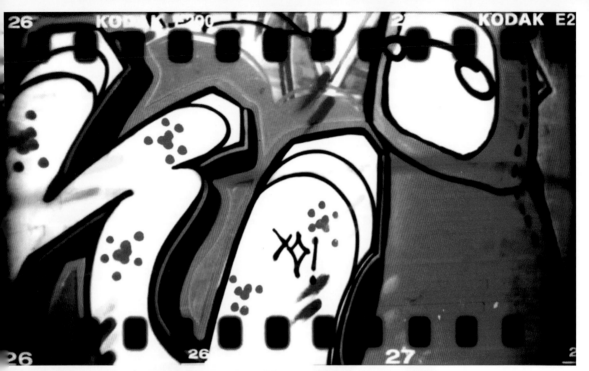

FISHEYE

Another modification for the Holga is to attach a removable fisheye lens to the already wide-angle lens of the Holga. This will create a nearly circular image on a square print. Get seriously close, fly low or hang high. It's all about angles when the fisheye is on and there is nothing that the 180 degree lens can't capture.
see: www.lomography.com/holga

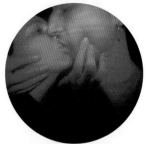

POLAROID

A Polaroid back has been designed for the Holga. Straightforward Polaroid's are an expensive habit.
But nothing can compare to the instant thrill of receiving a print seconds after taking a photograph.

Another beauty of Polaroid is the ability to create image transfers. The technique itself has been around for decades and consists of printing the Negative side of the Polaroid onto any surface. You will need to: take the shot, wait a few seconds, peel the Polaroid and discard the print. Place the negative of the Polaroid (that is usually thrown away) onto a sheet of paper for instance and gently rub it down. Wait a couple of minutes and peel it off slowly. The effect is, as always, unpredictable and truly stunning.

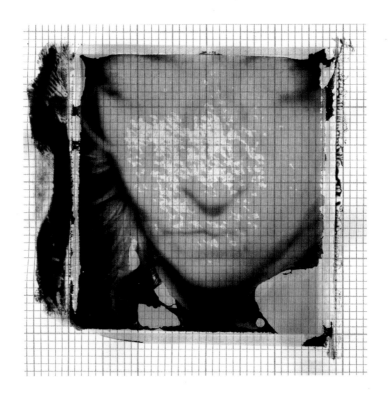

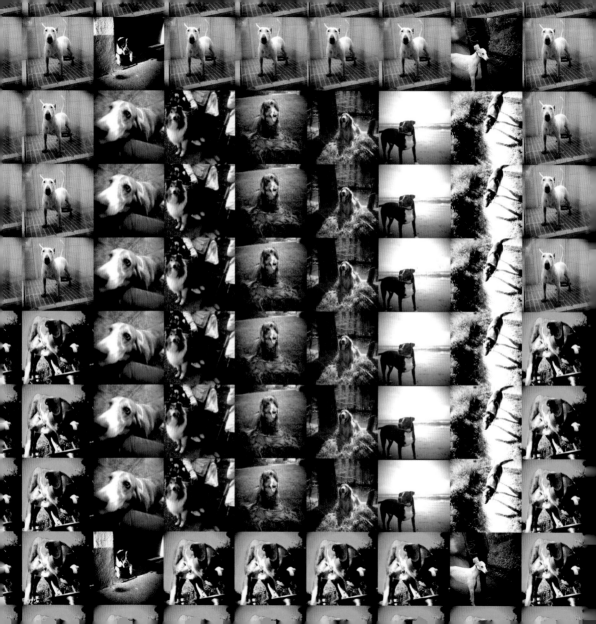

TIPS AND TRICKS

HOLGA

A GRAND SELECTION OF VALUABLE TIPS, WRITTEN BY THE
TRUSTWORTHY EXPERT MEMBERS OF THE lomography.com WEBSITE.
(VISIT THEIR LOMOHOMES AT lomography.com/homesDeLuxe)
CHECK OUT HUNDREDS MORE AT www.lomography.com/tips

DANDAN:
THE WOBBLE

"after you've finished the reel... and the the film is all wound up and out of the camera... gently unwind it a bit... kinda 'wobbling' it. IMPORTANT, don't do this too much or in full sun either or you'll have nothing left. it gives the best light leaks possible!!!"

TNT

DELEX:
4 COLOUR
EXPLOSIVE

"Click away on a subject 4 times but use different gels on your colourflash (120CFN Users it's easy) You get wicked overlapping colours and multiple poses (or faces!) in a shot..."

DECIBELL 72:
UP CLOSE &
PERSONAL

"A great way to get around the close focusing limitations of the Holga is to find an old, cheap close-up lens and tape it to the front of the Holga's lens. By testing the optimal distance for focus with a 35mm camera you can get pretty good results although a few rolls of film through the Holga is the best way to get the feel for your new, close focusing."

DALBERGARIA: LIFE PASSING BY

"A 100 ASA film or slower. A Holga with no flash. Somewhere to put the camera and keep shooting people passing by... Nice results."

ADAMSCOTT: 70MM HOLGA

"You'll need: two 120 film spools, tape, scissors, two rolls of 35mm film. A changing bag isn't big enough so use a pitch-black dark room. Tape the beginning of both rolls of 35mm film to the first 120 film spool and place into the winding part of the Holga. Go into the dark room and completely unwind all the film out of the 35mm cassettes and cut it at the end. Make sure you keep the beginning of the films in the winding part of the Holga as it can get messy. Find the end of the 35mm films and stick to the second 120 film spool. Wind all the film onto the second 120 film spool and place in the left part of the holga. Make sure the film viewer part on the back of the Holga is completely covered. All 35mm Holga rules apply e.g.: taping up the Holga and 30 to 35 clicks for each frame. When you've shot the film, go back to the lomo-pervert dark room, you'll need: two plastic film cases and silver foil. Open the back of the Holga and un-tape the 35mm film from the 120 film spools. Roll-up each film and place into separate film cases and cover the film cases with silver foil so no light can destroy your shots. Go to your lab and explain that the film is loose in the cases and tell them how to process it (negative or transparency) Good Luck!"

TNT

CYANWATER: HOLGA HORROR

"Place a red (or green) color gel over the flash. Take a pic of your friend with an eerie expression at somewhere dark or a dimly lit room (textured back-grounds will make the shot more interesting). Double-expose the frame with a normal portrait shot of another friend without the color gel. *If you already own the Color Flash Holga, all the better! Now, have fun scaring the shit outta your friends! :P
Tip: remember to frame your subjects on either side accordingly!"

ADAMSCOTT:
SHUTTERLESS

"Remove shutter in the holga. There are various ways of doing this and it can be a permanent modification. Do a search in google asking for 'holga modifications'. In these shots I used a separate flash in a blacked out room. The model would hold a light and as I wind the negative the light trails…"

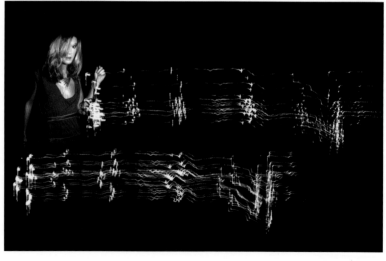

BONNIEPATTERSON: WORK YOUR HOLGAROIDS

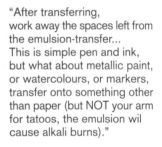

"After transferring,
work away the spaces left from
the emulsion-transfer...
This is simple pen and ink,
but what about metallic paint,
or watercolours, or markers,
transfer onto something other
than paper (but NOT your arm
for tatoos, the emulsion wil
cause alkali burns)."

DURRUTY_DE_ALBA: FLASH & SUN

"In spite of having great sun illumination, you could point and use the flash against the sun to avoid shadows..."

ERASERHEAD: SKIING

"The Holga loves the clear, crisp blue skies and bright snowy mountains you get on ski trips. Always take one with you and you'll be amazed at what can be achieved with 100 ASA"

JTUCK33:
MULTIPLE FILTERS

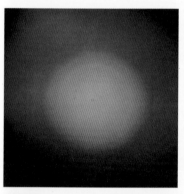

"Use a combination of colour filters and throw in a splash of colour flash (Holga Colour Flash) and get interesting images. User's choice for the colour combinations"

GOLDHAMMER: TRIPOD HOLGA

"For more sharpness and pinhole use, try: 'The Tripod Holga'. You will need 3 things: some superglue, a 1/4"x20 nut and a Holga camera. Put glue in the middle at the bottom of the camera. Place the nut in the glue. After a few hours, give the nut a second time of glue. Let it dry for 24 hours, and you can now mount it on a tripod."

JONCHERRY: BULB

"Use your Holga on Bulb setting with the flash. Find 2 cool mega interesting things to lomo. Shoot the first with the flash and instantly cover the lens wait for the flash to recharge then point and shoot at the other object or person and allow the flash to go off again! I feel that it works very well with people."

KHON_FUSED: HOLGA CFN B SETTING

"Remember to reset the Holga CFN's B setting back to N after shooting a long exposure image. Remember: Set B back to N! The first image taken one evening on B setting was deliberate. Remember - Set B back to N! The subsequent images taken the following day were not meant to be taken on B setting. Remember - Set B back to N! The rather dense negatives were still salvageable when scanning. Remember - Set B back to N! In some cases the results were quite engaging... but... Remember - Set B back to N! One telltale sign to look out for is your Holga CFN making a sound as though the shutter has been fired on the downwards press... Remember - Set B back to N! ...then making the same sound again as you release the shutter lever. Remember - Set B back to N! Just in case I failed to mention it... Remember - Set B back to N!"

TNT

JOHNNYHOLGA:
HOLGA FLASHING

"The flash on the Holga isn't as useless as it looks! Team it up with some x-processing and you get some really strong vignetting bringing you right into the picture. Its also useful as a fill in flash as shown in the image where the girl was shot with her head directly in front of the sun - I turned the flash on to make sure detail in the subject wasn't lost to a silhouette."

L_VAGNOZZI: DOUBLE IN TWO CITIES

"Buy a 35mm film, put it in your Holga and shoot your photo and roll up your film. PAY ATTENTION, and DON'T ROLL UP ALL THE FILM BUT LEAVE SOME CENTIMETERS OUT!!! After meet new Lomo Friends in other city. Send the exposed film at your Lomo Friends, and he should RE-Expose your film with his LCA...
Enjoy it!!!"

LADYM:
SAME PIC
DIFFERENT
POSITION

"shoot and shoot and shoot again on the same frame, even changing your colorflash!"

LURGEE:
B&W FILM

"Load a roll of pure b/w film into your Holga. Yes pure, not the ones which use C-41 to process. These are usually processed in the darkroom. You'll get really nice blacks and whites without the tinge of blues or pink. And of course, you'll get nicer grains."
;)

MARCOLITOS: SUPER GRAIN

"Try a 1600 ASA film or more for night shots or for taking pictures with very low light. Pictures look is quite drammatic and the grain is just superb. For the sample shots I used Ilford 3200."

MOLOTOVCOKETAIL: HOLGA SAMPLER

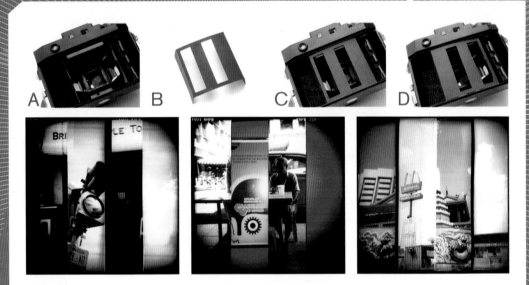

"Just follow these steps... A. Get a Holga and remove the "12 frame mask" B. Cut-out a mask like in the diagram with a piece of dark color cardboard C. Place it in your Holga before the film and shoot!! After you shoot the last frame, don't forward the film. Remove the film in a darkroom and wind it back for the second exposure D. Rotate the mask to the other side as in the diagram, load the previous film and start shooting again... and there are the results. Happy Holgaing... Oh, the credit goes to Xenin, too!"

MOLOTOVCOKETAIL:
PANORAMIC HOLGA

"To shoot a panoramic view of the whole stretch of building like the sample here... 1st, start from the left end... shoot the 1st frame (#1)... when you wind, don't use the reading at the rear window... count on the click. It's about 18 to 20 clicks... then point your holga to the right from the 1st frame... shoot the second frame... wind 18 to 20 clicks again... turn to the right... shoot the 3rd frame... after this, wind to frame #3 (If you start the 1st frame at #1) then turn to the right again and shoot the last frame. This is like you shoot 4 frames in the space of 3 frames. Here is the result!!"

NOT7HERE: SPOTLIGHTING

"Take your Holga to a party or other dark dreary area where people are out of their wits and use the white flash on your ColorFlash Holga to get some great vignetted shots. The images just pour out of the darkness; however make sure to remove the 6x4.6 mask for the best vignettes. Stay true to form: get your shots from the hip."

TNT
HOLGA

PALMERSTON: INTERACT WITH YOURSELF

"Everyone knows the 'dark place + flash' double exposure trick... The name speaks for itself... To make better self portraits like that, you've got to interact with yourself... The results are great and funny..."

REMITCH:
WATER DREAM

"Not really a tip... shoot a lake or a river with blue sky, turn the Holga upside down and repeat. Xpro, and voila! Dreamy isn't it ?"

RENATA_V: HOLE PUNCH PAPER MASK

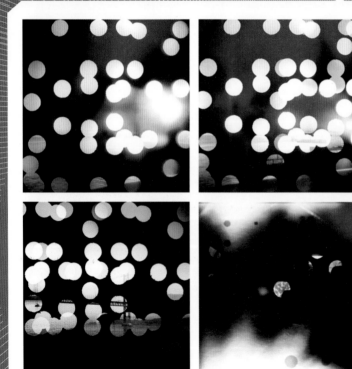

"Take the mask of your camera off. Cut a piece of hard paper with the same size (6.5 x 7cm). With a hole punch make as many holes as you like. (If you don't want holes you can try any other shape... Just cut it in the paper). With tape, stick the paper to the camera. Make sure that it doesn't move. Put the film as you always do (The film must be over the paper mask), close the camera and start shooting. Only the holes (or the shape you have chosen) will let the light enter... You will have little holes showing what you've shot! The world in holes... or holes in the world."

SEANMICHEL: HOLGA FILTERS

"Filters on my Holga shots are made as simply as taping a sheet of acetate over the lens. These shots were made with a dark red film."

SINE18:
180C 2XPOSE

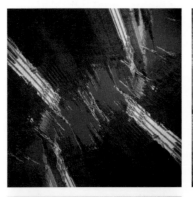

"Take one picture, turn the camera 180°, try to catch the same motif from the same angle and shoot again without advancing."

SKAC: LIGHT LEAKS

"Just mix (or hold it tightly) the film in the palm of your hands just before making it processed, I think this is the result of what I've done !!" :-)

SQIZO:
WINE TINTED
35MM HOLGA

"Put a 35mm roll in your Holga, but in the wrong side (invert the film position, the sensitive part of the film at the back), take your pictures, and you get wine colors on your pics, if you over-expose the film, the pics appear as a ghost golded pic."

MANDI: MACRO DISTANCE

"jealous of those top-down ground glass viewfinders? this divine WYSIWYG of SLR and TLR cameras? don't think! use the lomographic way! find some rastaman or weird looking guy out on the street, make a picture of him/her and ask for 1 or 2 long smoking papers. OCB or Rizla or any other brand. (slim or ultraslim if possible) NO this is not about drugs. but if you have some of your own, even better. i mean the papers! (?) open the back of your holga (make sure it is not loaded!). WET TONGUE ACTION! now stick the paper exactly where the film is supposed to be. set your holga on "B" mode and aim at a bright light thing. shade the back if the surrounding light is too bright. you can see the image appear on the paper. if you're using the macro-lense from the fisheye adaptor get as close as 4-5cm. tunnelvision macro: 3-4cm. get close until the image is really sharp. REMEMBER THE DISTANCE OR MEASURE IT. or both. remove papers, load film, find something interesting or boring, recall your brandnew distance know-how and go for it. set exposure time according to light. enjoy and share the results."

NSCHAPS: NIGHT SHOTS WITHOUT BULB

"If you are the owner of one of the older versions of the Holga (without the Bulb setting) then it is still possible to get night time shots exposed. try and find something to rest your holga on and simply keep releasing the shutter until your finger starts to hurt! Unless you're extremely delicate, you'll get a funky vibrating look."

NATALIE.ZWILLINGER: HAND WRITTEN TEXT

"WHILE DOING THE HOLGA POLAROID TRANSFER. WRITE ON THE BACK SIDE OF THE POLAROID WHILE IT IS STILL ON THE PAPER DEVELOPING. THIS IS WHAT HAPPENS... FUNKY ASS SHIT"

NATALIE.ZWILLINGER: LET THE LIGHT COME IN

"F**k the black duct tape. don't try and make the Holga a "normal" camera. the Holga is the Holga cause it's a f**king Holga."

ADAMSCOTT & SKAC: INTERNATIONAL HOLGA

"Shoot a film and get someone to shoot in between the frames. Once you receive an exposed film you need to re-wind the film onto a new spool. Do this in a dark room or changing bag and be careful as the negative is only stuck to the paper on one side. Load it up and shoot in between the frame numbers (around 15 clicks) You will end up with one HUGE International image... ENJOY!"

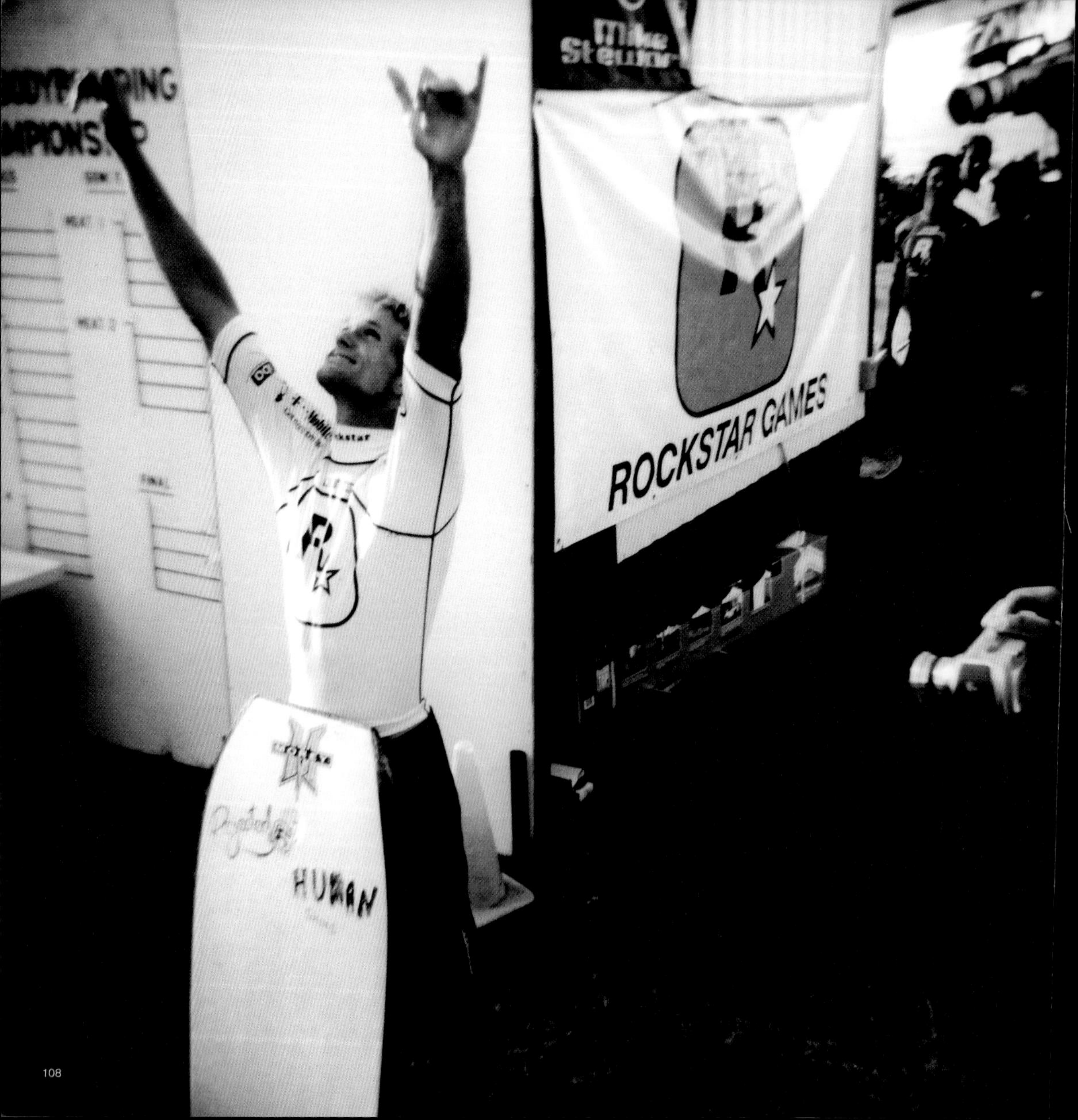
ROCKSTAR GAMES
HUMAN

PLEASE ALLOW ME TO PASS THE TORCH TO SOME OF THE BEST HOLGA SHOOTERS
WITHIN THE GLOBAL COMMUNITY OF LOMOGRAPHERS. KEEP A SHARP EYE READY FOR
THEIR SUSPENSEFUL LIFESTYLES, THEIR EXHILARATING SELF-WRITTEN BIOGRAPHIES
AND THEIR VARIED TESTIMONIALS AS TO WHAT MAKES THE HOLGA SO SPECIAL.
IF YOU WANT TO SEE MORE OF THEIR WORKS OR MAKE A MARRIAGE PROPOSAL,
CHECK OUT THEIR LOMOHOMES AT www.lomography.com/homesDeLuxe

TESTIMONIALS

LADYM

AKA Marian Garrido

hi! I'm Marian Garrido from Asturias, Spain, but i'm living in Barcelona from 4 months. I'm just turned into 21, and I'm studiying fine arts, but I'm graphic designer. and I just have to say that noise is for heroes!!

CHUO104

AKA Dario Alvarado

I was born in New York City on 28 August 1970 (The same day as Goethe). I live in Tokyo, Japan, where I work as an English teacher. I keep my sanity by writing poetry and taking photographs.

krebb

my holga is
as simple as I am.

self-taughtman

he's covered in
duct tape and makes
for great conversation.

OuroborosX

my plastic friend captures the world
like no other... and no two are the
same... the more i abuse it, the more
it responds with beautiful accidents...
there is nothing holga can't do, and
the world gets softer than a dream
through it's plastic eye...

karlbeck

even in the cold
she never gets frigid

VACLAVH

My name is Vaclav Ondrej Hasek and I am a citizen of the World.

Occupation: Slacker, Graphic Designer and Painter extraordinaire.
Current Location: Lafayette, Louisiana, but not limited to the deep
south, as the Holga factor is worldwide. Do I like 80's fashion? No,
but I do like to rock the Holga a la Rico Suave. Say it with me, RICO SUAVE.
Closeted passions: My growing leisure suit collection, the Lawrence
Welk Show, eating Boudin, and an extensive all girl Japanese pop-rock band vinyl
collection. Little known fact: The universe, if finite, is shaped like a donut.
Which is why the donut is the perfect food.

OPTICAL LENS

1:8 F=60mm

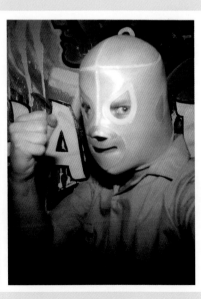

san_san

she is the boss and you cannot expect anything from her. but when she is in a good mood, she gives you pure beauty, it's up to her!

emay

like every good partner, she's low maintenance.

rebarbative

its easy and simple to use. it's chaotic in the results.

neve

plastic is fantastic. it's light and umbreakable, it's squared. but the thing that makes my holga so special is her name! me and my holga. every time i speak of her to someone new, male, they guess i have a beautlful friend and they ask to meet her! it's so funny

SINE 18

AKA Gesine Birgit Rudolph

Born in sweet '75, "Ich bin eine Berlinerin", now living in exile in Switzerland (Zurich), I try to make a living with science (currently I'm writing my PhD thesis in the field of microbiology), I'm a radical advocate of plastic- and medium format cameras (I am proud to be able to call myself owner of the HOLGA, an ancient Seagull TLR and the Colorsplash - the only digital camera I own is the one that came along with my mobile phone), I am a passionate but rather ungifted rider of boards on various surfaces (Snowboarding, Skateboarding, Windsurfing) I love good company and pub evenings but am, however, absolutely club-incompatible.

GOLDHAMMER

No real name known

Favourite music:	Kraftwerk
Favourite animal:	A Giraffe
Favourite photographer:	David Lachapelle
Favorite shoe brand:	Lakai
Favourite food:	Tom Yum Soup
Favourite car:	Citroen DS
Favourite day:	Thursday
Favourite color:	Indigo blue
Favourite phrase:	Your Holga will melt in a hot car
Favourite quote:	Make cows, not war.

SKAC

AKA Stephanie Kac

(Half french-Half slovenian)
26 years old girl living in Paris since ever!
Job: graphic designer. Second job: sleeper, dreamer and lomographer. Wait the whole year to spend the summer on a paradisiac island (Yeu Island) with my love Nicolas. Sun, seafood, friends and happiness and love: my cat, red whine, knitting scarves, shopping, Apple computer, psychoanalysis and lomography!

BRONWENHUG

AKA Bronwen Hughes

Screenwriter, filmmaker. NYC/LA/Toronto. My favourite way to take photos is to wander in some place on the globe where absolutely nothing is familiar. Smells, light, textures, faces. Everything is so new that my senses kick into hyper-alert. I become obsessed with capturing it all, to remember the experience for all time. Of course, there are also days when the familiar seems so alien that it provides the same fascination. Which means that I am almost never without a camera.

valayres

it's the most
amazing cheap
date i've ever had

ikhaan

it never complains...can stay
alone for weeks without
starving...is always ready to
go out...the perfect love
whenever you want :->

holer

the holga is a magical
camera. it does what it wants
to do with the subject i point
it at. i just point and click and
let my trusty holga do the rest

loetz

my holga was given to me as a birthday
present from my best friend and now
my holga is my new best friend. i never
go anywhere without this amazing
camera. it is always by my side ready
for my imagination and inspiration to
focus my eyes on the next shot.

DECIBELL72
A BIT ABOUT DEREK LEE BELL

I spend my days working as an assistant sound editor in Hollywood, California. Live better, work union. One month I rode in an elevator with Henry Rollins, Tyra Banks, Forrest Whitaker, Burt Reynolds and Angela Lansbury. I can often be found strolling up and down Hollywood Blvd on my lunch-hour taking lomographs of Midwestern tourists. My cats name is Lomo. I love to eat breakfast cereal morning, noon and night.

SQIZO

AKA Ignasi Perez-Noguera

i'm graphic and industrial designer and photo addict just a normal guy who try to life his dreams in this world

Just holgarize your WORLD!!!
BE FREE, NO RULES,
DREAM & ACT!!

BONNIE PATTERSON

About Me:

1. a registered nurse (RN) employed full time
2. favorite food: a Hot Hot Vindaloo
3. in love with the fragile plastic Holga, in awe of the Holga with a Polaroid back.
4. addicted to oxygen... breeeaaathe deep... ahhhhhhh, love it.
5. once played flute with a jazz band (only once, I''m not very good)
6. once gave Ewa Rudling a hug (outside Café Flore in Paris)
7. once played "Russian" martini challenge with a fellow lomographer, he won.
8. favorite cities are: Chicago U.S.A., NYC U.S.A., Paris, France and Vienna, Austria.
9. I've never been to Vienna or Austria.
10. went to law school and passed the bar exam... gonna be a lawyer when I grow up, but that's a long way off.
11. currently reside in Ann Arbor, Michigan U.S.A.

COSMONAUT

AKA Mauricio Arana

**I'm a graphic designer from Bogota DC, Colombia; I studied Visual Arts and Graphic Design. I work as a freelance designer and I am a college teacher, I expend all my free time (and money) taking pictures. I have two cats and two turtles, I like to hang out with my friends and I LOVE my girlfriend. I like to photograph people; my friends, strangers, myself, my girlfriend, anyone. But I shoot everything that catches my eye. I think anything can be a good subject for a photo just if you want it, if you feel it. My frustrated dream is to be a musician.

OUROBOROSX

AKA Liad Cohen

I live in New York City and manage the group Ours, who are releasing their third record on Geffen Records in early 2006. I used to be a children's book editor for Sesame Street for 4 years. I've traveled to 20 countries, and have been to 48 states in the US. I have over 500 Radiohead songs in my iTunes, because i collect their live and rare recordings like they hold the answers to all of life's questions. My dream is to one day publish (and naturally first complete) my novel, and to make a living taking photographs. I wear black T-shirts at least 5 days a week. I like to walk everywhere. I need new shoes.

OLDBEN

AKA Ben Deering, for the uninitiated...

born in the 70's, survived all the glorious 80's, even with clothes like these....
a little plastic tragic, i tend to get carried away with my lack of need for a viewfinder, in fact, most times it's covered with black tape. living south of the equator means my christmas is HOTTER than most lomographers. inspiration comes in the form of coopers pale ale, green grass, red scooters, pasties with sauce, cricket, planes, travel, my beautiful girl and our three crazy chihuahuas.

OPTICAL LENS

1:8 F=60mm

1:8 F=60mm

OPTICAL LENS

SBG1

AKA Shane Goguen

Occupation: Photographer.
Three years ago while deciding on darkroom classes at my local community college I noticed a course devoted to a plastic camera that has 'its own unique vision'. I picked out my darkroom class but didn't forget about the camera. Soon after I bought one and fell in love with the results. Three years and four Holgas later I am still at it, loving every blurry vignetting image I create with it.

martinroe

totally unpredictable so it's always exciting to get my films developed as i never know what i'm gonna get

antsnf

she never complains when we're on the road to who knows where in this amazing world.

snapshotartifact

it casts a little bit of film magic over dull reality.

eraserhead

it looks like a toy, it feels like a toy, but no toy i know can turn out pictures like the holga. you never know whats gonna come out of the other end

HOLGA

1:8 F=60mm

OPTICAL LENS

JBENINATO

AKA Jill Beninato

I am a pet photographer/artist from Virginia Beach, VA. I fell in love with photography when I was 15 years old and have been making photographs ever since.
My adult life in a nutshell... I met a guy... I got married... we bought a house... we got a dog... liked him, so got another dog... had a child... got a bigger car... moved... got a bigger house... got another dog... watched hurricane Katrina on CNN... wanted to help... adopted a fourth dog abandoned after hurricane... no more dogs... need a kennel license for five... husband will divorce me... After my family and dogs of course, photography is my favorite thing. The first time I used my Holga camera I was hooked. That has led to a pin hole Holga, a fisheye camera and a lens baby. In this digital age, which I am guilty of joining, there is still no replacement for my cheap plastic cameras. They remind me to be an artist first and that life is full of things out of our technical control. My style is 'casual bohemian' with a dash of dog hair. I love classic rock and alternative music, travelling whenever possible, and experiencing new things. My Holga reminds me to shoot from the hip from time to time, in all aspects of life. Thanks for selecting my photographs for the book...I can't wait to see the final results... You guys beat me to the punch..I have been playing around with a book idea called 'Holga Hounds' using my Holga pet photos. You probably just saved me a lot of money...

joncherry

when it's very sunny
and hot my holga
always wears sun
cream.

mandi

it's so well-tempered!
shots turn out to look
fantastic even if you
expected it to look like
a pile of dog-gaga

vincent.rose

my holga takes my joy and
keeps it on a roll inside.
the only way to get it back
is to develop the film and
put it on paper.

waind

looking at my holga, i'm surprised
not by the photos it takes, but by
the fact that it takes any pictures at
all! it's the downtrodden working
class hero - the underdog of the
medium format world.
i like underdogs.

goon

i love how people dont care too much about what you're photographing - when your camera looks like you stole it off your little sister.

milchtrinken

she fits into no pocket.

brianmilo

the way people look at you when you're shooting with a taped up plastic toy

gravityroom

the holga is so lo-fi, so dirty, so plastic, so beautiful!

HOLGA

AKA Cindy Tan

My eyes are like the shutter of a camera but I don't have a photographic memory. I love the Holga but my life is never square! A starving photographer and struggling writer, my dream is to publish a book whereby I could open up through pictures and words. Inspire the world's famous photographers and the folk next door. Cameras, caffeine and chums - they are what made up the facts of my life!

MANDI

AKA Manfred Steininger

It's all part of the game, we're all players of the game sharpen your senses!

1:8 F=60mm

OPTICAL LENS

CLARISSEMERIGEOTØ

AKA Clarisse Mérigeot

What's the point, after all, of having 10 fingers if you can't use one of them at least for pushing a plastic button instead of completely devoting them to naughty deeds? Legend says that after counting them, Clarisse Mérigeot discovered that she in fact had exactly 20 fingers. She figures, why not use them for something less nasty than usual? while her other fingers are typically preoccupied with more important and one could say dirtier tasks, her right index finger is content with pressing the small plastic shutter button on her Holga camera, birthing her vast photo collection. A bit self-conscious, she never finds herself pretty enough even though Yann Le Corre apparently thinks she's wonderful. But is that good enough and who is Yann Le Corre, by the way? Working as a journalist in Paris, France, Clarisse is the tragically fantastic outcome of successful bourgeois education. As a naturally maniacal and relentless photographer, she often shoots, or rather portraits her entourage always at less-than-convenient moments (otherwise what fun would it be?). What in the world could be funnier than making people fools of themselves? she ponders. A home is not a place, she says (this quote she read somewhere and of course made her own), ...a home is where lomographers are, holgagraphers as well. A home is a picture that you take and like. A pictures that reflects you or, better yet, makes you look more beautiful than you actually are. One surely cannot speak of Clarisse without mentioning that photographically speaking she owes everything to Liad Cohen, who she likes to call master not because it turns him on, but because he kindly took her on as his young padawan.

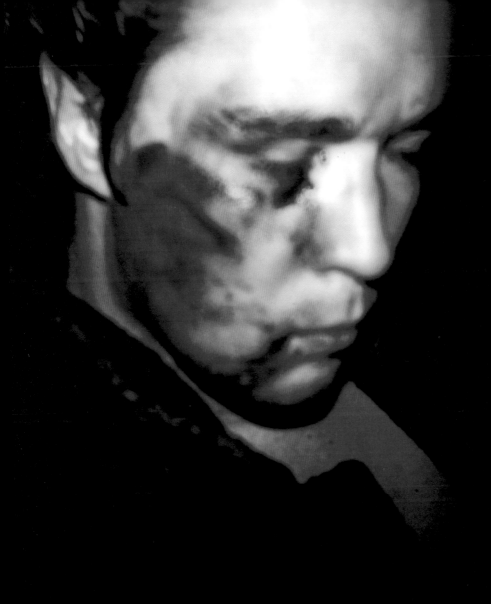

londonhair

she has magical powers

jonee

the holga is anti-technology! it produces images with soul; images strikingly different to the sterile, pin-sharp, perfectly-exposed digital shots that we seem to be suffocated with these days.

kenzitaka

expect the unexpected

bmxedd

frustrating, unpredicatable, it can be a massive high or a big low depending on whether your pictures come back.

SNAPSHOTARTIFACT

AKA James Felder

Some info about me:
I'm a writer for TV, movies, and eccentric other media.
I'm a founding member of the NYU Bagpipe Band.
My photographic heroes are Henri Cartier-Bresson, Robert Capa,
and Weegee. My friends, family, and random strangers are very gracious
and patient to let me steal moments of their lives as pictures.
You can see a new snapshot of my life every day at
www.SnapshotArtifact.org! (note it's *org* not *com*)

OPTICAL LENS

1:8 F=60mm

JOHNNYHOLGA

I am a London based graphic designer, toiling away for corporate clients by day and trying to be a more creative superhero at night... current world domination projects involve designing badges and T-shirts.
I love the randomness of the Holga, especially when teamed with the un-predictability of cross processing, achieving things that would take hours on a computer and making the wait for every set of pictures an exciting surprise, just like a Kinder egg! I also enjoy the odd looks you get when using the Holga, I'm sure people think its a joke camera and are waiting for the water to squirt in their face. My favorite pet would be a monkey, I would teach it how to use a camera and send it up tall buildings.

OPTICAL LENS

∏EVE

I'm just a girl in the world. 23 years old, i'm studying photography at the European Institute of Design in Milan. My favourite pet is my stereo, i cannot live without music. i cannot live without art. and i love snow... those little and delicate frozen stars. (My lomo nik name NEVE in Italian means snow) LA NEIGE, incredible natural poetry... i think life should be lived as poetry. My story: one day i was floating around my city, dreaming with open eyes as always... when i saw a plastic toy camera in a shop window! what the hell is this Holga? It was very cheap, so i bought it and i start shooting everything! Wow... I fell in love with this plastic fantastic medium format arm of communication! And i realize that photography would become my life. and so be it.

OPTICAL LENS

1:8 F=60mm

NSCHAPS

AKA Neil Chapman

Born 1979 in Basildon, Essex (England), went to school and college, left, travelled around the World a bit; USA, Canada and the East Coast of Australia. Realising I couldn't afford to travel around forever without a job, I went home and decided to work on getting a career that would pay me to travel. I wanted to be a Photographer and travel the World, and one year later it hit me; join the Royal Air Force as a Photographer! So I did and here I am... in sunny Scotland. I eat, sleep and drink photography, and my Holga plays a big part in that. You never really know what you're going to get from it. It never fails to suprise me and that's why I'll always own and cherish it.

KHON_FUSED

AKA Phillip Allen

I teach cinematography to computer animation students and plug some of the gaps in my time with enjoyment of stills photography. With the immanent arrival of our first child the amount of time spent behind the camera is bound to increase exponentially! My wife and I have been avid users of Lomographic type cameras since we married and I bought her a LCA whilst she bought me my first Holga. Having worked with digital media for many years the raw, sometimes brutal tactile immediacy of the Holga proved highly refreshing and the mode of working that seems to overtake one in using a Holga has gone on to inform work that I undertake digitally. The Holga is a camera that makes perfection of flaws and it is that spirit that I hope to carry through into any of my work regardless of the tool at hand.

JTUCK33

AKA Joe Tucker

I make a living lending people money to buy homes. Though I take photos as often as I can, most of my free time is taken up by my 3 year old son and 1 year old daughter. Combine them with Daisy the dog and Lucy the Cat (not to mention my loving wife) and my days are always filled. I grew up in Michigan and Pennsylvania and now live in Atlanta. We are intowners---an urban pioneering family---and would not have it any other way and love taking advantage of all the city has to offer. I have had more than a casual interest in photography since college and discovered my Holga just before my son was born. Holga On!

PRIMEOBJECTIVE

AKA Chris Keenan

I'm a Photographer, Film Maker and VJ addicted to the beauty and cinematic nature of Holga photography. I love Lomography in general and have been involved in the scene for a few years. Putting on Lomo shows in the city of Birmingham and encouraging others to get excited about all things Lomo. Super 8 Cameras are another passion of mine. I own three and shoot Super 8 whenever I get the chance. I make short Super 8 films, I entered the Straight 8 film festival this year and my film 'Fidget' was selected and screened at 291 Gallery in London. A fair few of my Holga Shots have helped me pay the bills and fed the hunger for more 120 film. My personal archive of Super 8 acts as a source material for live visual (Vj) performances. My favourite band right now is BABY ROSEBUD from New Orleans. They're so cinematic and inspire me to make films. The Mandolin is my instrument of choice and has won me great notoriety. For some reason I'm attracted to difficult and quirky women, perhaps that explains the love affair with Holga.

OPTICAL LENS 1:8 F=60mm

L_VAGNOZZI

I'm Luigi, known as L_VAGNOZZI in lomography. I'm 27 years old, and I come from Roseto degli Abruzzi, a little town in front of Adriatic Sea and near Pescara. At the moment I'm a Student of Architecture at Politecnico di Torino, so I live here in Torino! I'm at the end of study... I hope to get degree this next summer! After I hope to get married with Roberta, my girlfriend! Don't worry... I'll put in Lomography all the pics about the wedding album! I have also a mistress: HOLGA!!! At the moment my girlfriend isn't jealous, we will see! I love also the visual arts, I love travelling, but I hate the airplanes! Each time I fly, I become the more anxiety man of the world! I don't know why... I love also the music from the 70's, rock progressive, (Pink Floyd, Yes, King Crimson, Emerson Lake and Palmer), but also the classical music, the jazz (my favourite artist is Keith Jarret, and Miles Davis), and the contemporary music: from Radiohead to Belle and Sebastian, from REM to Alanis Morrisette, from Tom Waits to Nick Cave!!! I hear a lot of music, I'm lucky cause I can study, draw and listen to the music at the same time!!! I love too the movie! My favourite director is KRZYSZTOF KIESLOWSKI! I love all his film! And the my favourite is the BLUE FILM!!! I wasn't the same after to see this film! Mi favourite actors are Juliette Binoche, Al Pacino, Woody Allen, Marcello Mastroianni, Marlon Brando, Robert De Niro... What I love about the lomography is internationalities! People from all the word who love the photography and get experiments with film, camera and filters! Visual communication: I think to get my thesis with this theme! I'm that. No more!

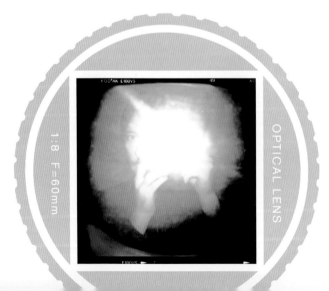

OPTICAL LENS — 1:8 F=60mm

DOMINO

AKA John Eldridge.

This is just a part of my life, this spontaneous analog image snatching. This is just a part of what floats me. Other branches of my everyday movement affect my created imagery: Surfing, Music, Life, Dreams. I shoot what I see as I tread my path, without pre-conceived notion or ideal. Give me plastic eyes any day. When my finger is not on the plastic button you'll find me sliding around on ironing boards in the sea (some call it surfing), loving a girl, being somewhat of a freelance multimedia professional and director of a small revivalist surfboard company. Generally I'm a dreamer.

JONHESLOP

AKA Jon Heslop

I'm currently studying physics at University College London [UCL]. Lomography is the überbomb; it consumed me back in November 2004. I have used embossing tape to stick the phrase 'physics rocks my world' onto the back of my holga. I love music my favourite band are Radiohead, I'm also heavily into post-rock. There's nothing better than a good old cheese toastie with Worcester sauce. My aim is to document [with photos] as much of God's creation as I possibly can. When I have kids, I'm gonna buy them cameras and tell them to take pictures of things they think are important, it'd be so interesting. I really wanna get into instant holgaroid action.

1:8 F=60mm — OPTICAL LENS

CARMENDEVOS

AKA Carmen Devos

I am an office mouse with an entire world in my head and a smile on my face when I'm escaping and heading to the stars. I want to see, to learn, to feel, to fly if possible. I document my life on pictures. I am obsessed, don't want to miss any details. I like to share, to participate but I also need time on my own, a lot. My head is like a merry-go-round, filled with unfinished thought and a lot of chaos. I sleep too little cause there is so much I want to do in a day. I live fast, at high speed. I travel, watch movies, laugh, laugh a lot, love my family, like to be spoiled. I am a gamer and never too tired for some competition, I love quizzes, can't count, love to know, love so much...

OPTICAL LENS

SEANMICHEL

AKA sean duncan

time challenged architect, venice california

1:8 F=60mm

OPTICAL LENS

BLACKPOT

AKA Jim Stewart

Five Random Jesse Blackpot facts:
- Favourite treat: Kenny's Juicy Twists.
- Cannot pronounce 'daiquiri'.
- When operating heavy machinery he's more wired than a Christmas tree.
- He has no nose hair. None.
- Is not available by subscription.

OPTICAL LENS

1:8 F=60mm

NATALIE.ZWILINGER

AKA NATALIE ZWILINGER

I THINK MY OCCUPATION IZ A LONG TERM STUDENT. I HATE TO SAY IT BUT I HAVE NOT BEEN TAKING FOTOZ IN THE PAST MONTHS. DONT ASK ME WHY. A VIRUS MAYBE. I MAINLY HAND PRINT SILKSCREEN IMAGEZ OF MY PHOTOZ ON CLOTHES THEZE DAYZ. A TEXTILE FUTURE MAYBE. I LOVE THE 80'S. THE MUSIC ROCKS. AND THE FASHION SENSE WAS SO UGLY IT HAS TO BE ONE OF THE GREATEST TIMEZ OF ALL. THE HOLGA IS MY FAV AFTER THE LC-A. POLAROID TRANSFER IS MY ADDICTION. THE FACT IT IS A SIMPLE PLASTIC BOX. NOT TOO INTELLIGENT IN ITS FEATUREZ. MAKES IT SIMPLY BRILLIANT. I LOVE CATS. CATS ARE MY LIFE. I THINK I WAS A CAT IT MY PAST LIFE. WISH I COULD GET MARRIED AND HAVE BABYZ WITH A CAT. THAT COULD BE PERFECT!!!

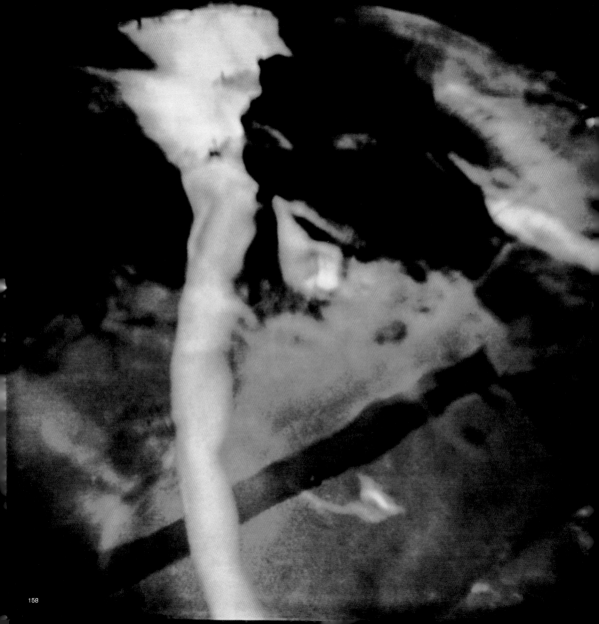

REMITCH

AKA Rémi

I come from Paris. Now I'm studying urban planning, I'm a member of the fellowship of the Holgarian Plastic Beauty. When my hands are not stuck on my plastic lover, I like to build pieces of lousy house music on my computer or play the guitar with the wonderful JazzyFunkySoulishRock band, MAIS 69 or hit the very distorted bass of the unique jazz punk band of the galaxy, LORENZO & THE LAMAS (what a nice name, hum hum...). I like stupid and fast sports like skateboarding and snowboarding, and editing videos. By the way, I'm a civil engineer too. All those occupations may one day lead me directly into schizophrenia... Plastic fantastic, shooting with holga is like playing "Duck Hunt" on the NES with this crappy orange plastic fake gun. By the way, my favourite Radiohead song is fake plastic trees, coincidence? Lots of Lomo love for everyone, see you in Paris!

JON CHERRY

I am currently in France doing mission work in a city called Perpignan.
Back home in England i work as a Swimming Teacher and Car Rally
Photographer. When i arrive home in July 2006 i hope to study at a London
University doing Photography, also i will hopefully be working closely with
a band called Stateless there too. I spend my time in Perpignan working
in a church, lomoing, generally kicking around and befriending homeless
people. I prefer fashion from the 1950's and my favourite pet would have
to be an Otter!

1:8 F=60mm

OPTICAL LENS

SEVERIN

AKA Severin Matusek

I study philosophy in Vienna and I try to be an actor every now and then. I recently tried to write poetry in an airplane and I am sometimes a wild guy when I take the public transport without having a valid ticket. I like to sing to midi karaoke versions of Beatles songs and I am the co-founder of the Jelly dance. As a child I wanted to become a tap dancer.

SHANTI929

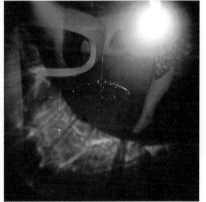

I'm currently working in the Children's museum as a project executive, and still expecting more new challenges on my job. Usually I wander around the city in most of my leisure time. If I could have more time to spare, I would love to spend the whole afternoon at the shore for just hearing the sound of the beautiful ocean. I have a pet turtle and a puppy at the moment, love the calmness of my turtle, and on the other hand my puppy is the best wander partner. In conclusion, I, Myself, is an extreme: I love both black and white; calm and clamor; resplendence and mediocrity. Less talk, more imagine. I am, shanti chang!

fphilippeaux

holga is made in plastique. holga is so large. holga is really not easy to put in a pocket or a travel bag. holga is not discrete. holga does not look like a professional camera. but holga gives us, with such generosity, such beautiful images! i love holga!!!

hogwong

the holga is made in hong kong - just like me!

moominsean

it shows me what the world should look like.

jbeninato

i fell in love with my holga after the first roll of film. i love the dreamy, haunted quality of the photos, as well as, the unpredictable results.

NEJA

AKA julia svetlova

I'm global trotter, truly cosmopolit person, love to move around, see everything through the prism of my tatarian eyes; cinema addicted, books lover; heart in fire, funky groover; i'm the the ghost of hermitge {working in the photo store inside the famous hermitage museum, there i got to work after i became madly obsessed with taking lomos}; i adore summertime and believe that the things which don't kill us, make us stronger! and i'm crazy about colours and style! my fave pet is BELUGA and DOLPHIN, i think they are smartest creatures on earth! as for the fashion of 80's, i prefer the fashion of 1920's, and 1950-70's! these are really stylish epochs! but if by chance holga was created in 1980's, i love it, no matter when and where it was made!

007-0815-STYLER

AKA David Wilms

I am a photographer & lomosaphien in this world, never met another world so thatzzz it. I rather forget my keys when I/Elvis left the building, than one of my camerazzz. I am a german, blonde, male, 28 years old Styler, sometimes cute and sometimes angry.
I am a professional photographer, as I know. I love the fact that I always move between the real world (where I have to make money and pay my bills) and my own little stylish world (where I often try not to think just to shoot or to exist). If I like the fashion of the 80s? I dont really know, whether the fashion is from the 80s, 90s or 30s, itzzz good if it is in my wardrobe. I don't care about dating things to a special category. Today I like the fashion of the 80s, maybe tomorrow I hate it. My favorite pet is a turtle, because I've got 2 of them (Frisbee and Muffin) for almost 10 years. It seems to be that God is an artist that has created such interestingly beautiful beings. They look so extraordinary and nice, woah! God save the Queen, 007-0815-Styler and the holga book.

ERASERHEAD

AKA Greg Limna

I am a child trapped in a mans body, or is that a man trapped in a child's body, I'm not sure. I find things either really dull and boring or incredibly fun and exciting, there is no middle ground. When I find things that are fun and exciting I have to indulge myself until I'm full, or start to find these things dull and boring. The one subject I never find dull and boring are the weird and wonderful shapes and colours mother nature produces. I really love flowers, so vibrant and eccentric, sun flowers especially. What a marvellous imagination to design so many variations. And if I can capture these with my plastic friendly Holga then I am in ecstasy!!! Oh, did I tell you what I do for a living, I build sewers. Dull and boring or fun and exciting, you decide...

LONDONHAIR

AKA Laura Burlton

I am married and have two beautiful, creative, and photogenic daughters. I like to read fairytales. Sometimes, before I go to sleep, I check under the bed and in the closets for monsters. In the daytime, I run an e-commerce company that sells professional hair products. I am a licensed hairdresser but I hate to do hair. I take at least two cameras everywhere. I spend lots of time in the darkroom and I love to print my own photos. I used to want to be a rock star and was once the singer in a band, but we broke up before we ever performed live. I almost always wear black and have for over twenty years. My favorite city is New Orleans.

weezerine

it's mine and it's the
only one i have!

jenv101

it changes your
perception

sandstep

she's the most popular of all my
strange optics, in fact she makes
them all jealous. especially that
halloween when a pair of plastic
partners (working, mind you)
became a part of my costume.
i was the photojournalist from
apocalypse now.

mimimalism

it's so light you can
take it anywhere...

HOLGA

AKASARURU

AKA Laura Höll

a post-modern vegetarian with nomadic tendencies and the hots for olives who is searching for her mind.

VALAYRES

AKA Val Ayres

I am a 33 year old graphic designer/art director from Rio de Janeiro, Brazil. I am a self-confessed techno and samba lover. I breath art and am addicted to cinema. I studied in school at sdsu, California for 4 years, went back to Brazil and started working mostly within the music industry designing cd covers till 3 years ago, when i moved into corporate being hired by a big ad agency. I realized that big and corporate just didn't do it for me, I needed the freedom to create and now I am back on a freelance status looking forward to opening a small studio. Perhaps this search for freedom is also evident in my photography, where I am always using my cameras to document the little details of the world around me. By the way... Looking at the world through the lens of my camera is one of the things that makes me happy! =)

NOT7HERE

AKA Christopher Morgan Scullion Carter

Age: 23 1/2. Hometown: BibleBelt, Tennessee.
Current town: Boston, Massachusetts.
Interesting name fact: *Scullion*
means *bastard kitchen servant*
Profession: Clinical Social Worker in training
(in this case a therapist for a severely mentally
ill population), amateur Holganographer.
Personal Quote: "I aspire to having all of the
passion and none of the organization".
Me: struggling altruist, indefinitely definite
academic, western-shirt aficionado, grammer
hound, secretly angry with the world, banjo
player, indie rock music snob. Home page:
www.myspace.com/wookiesdancetothis

PALMERSTON

AKA Sávio Palmerston

I graduated in advertising, and used to work
with motion graphics. Now, I'm just trying to
start my own business and to stop biting my
nails. I want to learn the best way to approach
strangers for getting them to let me take their
photograph. I can't ride a bike. I make stupid
hair styles with soapy hair. I only wear
Chuck Taylor All Stars. I don't know
how to describe myself!

primeobjective

my plastic partner is chunky yet weighs
next to nothing, older than me yet has a
youthful, simple view of the world. always
offering unexpected surprises either filled
with joy or sorrow. my partner sometimes
takes a tumble and exposes themself but
of course this is allowed and brings delight
to everyone's eyes. to put it simply, my
partner is the best plastic friend and has
helped make dreams a reality.

bloodlight

coz
it's not a camera,
it's a magic box!

okok

it's so simple, but so
hard to figure out.

scootiepye

holga is
the ultimate chunky dream,
boxed in a black plastic
brick...

1:8 F=60mm

OPTICAL LENS

SCOOTIEPYE

AKA Helen Errington

Occupation: humanoid hardcore visual artist (female) with my own
hair and teeth. I have a plastic passion that extends beyond cameras -
but I'm not going into that right now *grins* I spend my time day-dreaming,
shooting lomo, and attending to my very small collection of Pooka's...
Life f a c t s > I Like: roast chicken, jaffa cakes, green swimming goggles, red socks,
tequila, expired film, white rabbits, chocolate ice cream, sundays, B movies, flippers,
window seats, & cheese. I Dislike: ironing, lipstick, snot, pineapples, hovering, green
peas, short-haired hamsters, twisted knickers, rules, yappy dogs & bingo. I once held
the school record for 100m with a time of 11.3 seconds. I can eat 72 jumbo fish
fingers. I rarely brush my hair. I drink cider & black. I can not play the violin. I dance
like an electric one legged chicken on a skate board. I can kill an eel. I speak in
strange tongues. I like to walk at night in the rain.
Lomographic Ambassador

DALBERGARIA

AKA Alexandre d'Albergaria

A compulsive contradiction collector.?
A Brazilian that doesn't like football.
A lover of photography who hates pictures.
A faithful man who doesn't
believe in monogamy.
A Romantic without believing in love.
A liar who always speaks the truth.
That's me: in passion today,
in passion everyday. After all,
something needs to be coherent.

OPTICAL LENS

1:8 F=60mm

I'm a thirty-one year old self-employed artist, designer, maker, photographer living in the North East of England. Most of my time at work is spent designing and producing one-off art installations for practicing artists. My own artwork is cross-disciplinary including video production, furniture making, performance and photography. Out of work I'm into all things retro - cine and sideboards, vinyl and vintage, antiques and anologue. Digital photography is an absolute no no - keep it retro, keep it romantic, keep it real!

goldhammer

it melts in a hot car

mikkelwurtz

she's so light and easy to cope with. i got her 3 years ago - and we have been together since.

ringo_fyre

using a holga is very much like making love to a beautiful woman - you've got to handle her gently, talk to her sweetly, and use plenty of duct tape.

french_for_hi-hat

it's inner beauty...

LURGEE

AKA Aloysius Lim

I fix airplanes by day and am a dreamer/slacker/sleeper/wannabe photographer whenever I'm not at work. I spend most of my free time with my girlfriend who's also an avid lomographer. Whenever we are not out taking photos, we just hang out and do stuff that most couples do. I don't have any pets. I've got no time for them! Maybe next time? Back in April 2003 when I was on long medical leave due to a knee surgery when I stumbled upon photos online which grabbed my attention. I only knew they were taken with lomos so I searched online and found out about lomography. A few weeks later, I bought a LC-A. It was good as I was able to pass my time as I was still on medical leave. Hehe. After a couple of rolls, I was hooked and never looked back. When did you get the Holga? The Holga was the next camera I got after the LC-A. Again, I saw interesting square photos online which I thought were cool and learnt that they were taken with the Holga. Went to the local store to get more information about it and the store had only 1 last piece of Holga left. The storeowner told me the next shipment would take weeks, I said "Alright, give me the last Holga and some films to start with!"

JILLOG

AKA Jill Pichocki

I am currently earning my MFA in photography while in Virginia. I work at a small camera shop that has been around since 1915. Lomography has become somewhat of an obsession and I carry my holga with me wherever I go. Asides from being a strong and faithful Christian, photography is my next passion. Last year I purchased a Polaroid back for my Holga and this has only fueled the fire for my love of this piece of plastic. I am also a member of polanoid.net which is another outlet to show off my Holgaroids. It is such a brilliant tool for creating beautiful images. My holga is a constant companion and sticks with me throughout all of my endeavors. Whether it is going to Japan to visit my brother or simply taking a long ride throughout the country this camera is always there. It has taught me so much about the wonderful possiblities of working with film and is a constant reminder as to how much film needs to stick around in this digital age.

DELEX

AKA leon della bosca

my name is leon, i love my holga,
i am a humanist i love my dog, dexter and my
girlfriend, lulu. life is art, lomo is beautiful...
i am a graphic designer from melbourne, australia.
i spend my time wasting it. i don't like fashion from
the 80's but i like the music. my dog dexter is more
than my favourite pet, he's my little buddy! my life
revolves around art and design, so i guess you
could say i live and love my work [not my own
work, just what i do for work]. insight: man rarely
has the courage to permit what he truly knows.
i love philosophy, that is my religion. bill hicks is
my god. i have faith in humanity yet humanity has
little faith in itself. oooooooooh, is that stirring
enough for you?

Born in Guadalajara, México
in the revolutionary year of 1968.
Physicist by Universidad de Guadalajara, graduated the
same day of the electron 100 anniversary. Actually working
at the Astronomy and Meteorology Institute there, mainly
in history and popularisation activities. Enjoy all
photographic soviet technology and former Mir publisher
books. Photography fan since eight years old, but late
captured lomographer in 2004. Lomo of the month in
www.lomographic.net in August 2004 with "Livertrain".
User of the day (March 08, 2005) in SETI@home.
Good coffeholic!!!

MOLOTOVCOKETAIL

AKA Yang Dar Yang

I am a graphic designer, art director and illustrator with lots of hobbies. My first hobby is drawing. I have been drawing since I was young, even before I know how to spell the word "draw". When I'm growing up, more and more interesting hobbies keeps coming to me... toys, gaming, photography, design, painting, reading, movie, music, diving, travel... then, one day, I saw these square pictures, with the strong vignette and leak effects... It strike my heart.. I told myself, this is what I'm going to shoot. I get myself one of this lovely piece of plastic, then we started our amazing journey together....

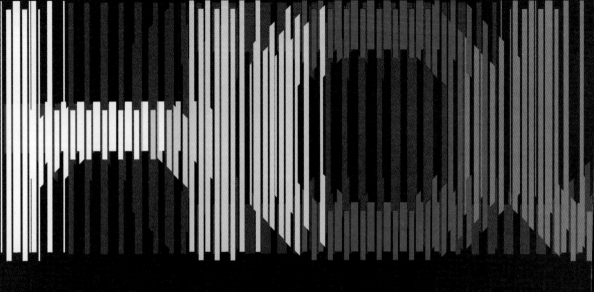

LINKS AND
FURTHER READING

www.meltingpop.it
www.toycamera.com

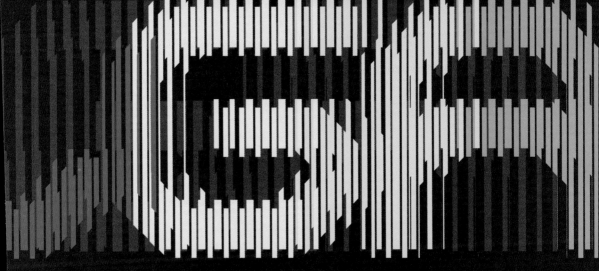

THANKS

Special thanks to Angelo Semeraro for previous designs and Jim Stewart for concept development, previous initial designs and the fantastic idea of melting a Holga. I would also like to thank the four Ms at Lomography, Manfred Steininger, Markus Wegscheider and Michael Kuhle for all their help throughout this project and Matthias Fiegl for allowing as much creative freedom as humanly possible. Finally, I must thank all the hundreds of contributors for submitting their fantastic Holga images for the book.

CONTRIBUTORS

username	lomohome	first name	last name	country-iso
007-0815-Styler.de	www.lomohomes.com/007-0815-Styler.de	David	Wilms	DE
adamscott	www.lomohomes.com/adamscott	Adam	Scott	GB
A-Doo	www.lomohomes.com/A-Doo	Ana	Dunjic	YUG
akhsarual	www.lomohomes.com/akhsarual	Laura	Hoell	GB
anttanant	www.lomohomes.com/anttanant	Darren	Ellis	US
antsnf	www.lomohomes.com/antsnf	Anthony	Olayon	US Hawaii
atomic762	www.lomohomes.com/atomic762	Jason	Randolph	US
bastet.lomo	www.lomohomes.com/bastet.lomo	Valentina	Cinelli	IT
blackpot	www.lomohomes.com/blackpot	Jim	Stewart	GB
bloodlight	www.lomohomes.com/bloodlight	Marie-Eve	Moretti	FR
blub03	www.lomohomes.com/blub03	Martin	Hueber	DE
bmxedd	www.lomohomes.com/bmxedd	Edward LC	Jung	GB
boku	www.lomohomes.com/boku	Pittaya	Sroilong	TH
branham	www.lomohomes.com/branham	Grant	Edwards	US
brianmilo	www.lomohomes.com/brianmilo	Brian	Milo	US
bronwenhug	www.lomohomes.com/bronwenhug	Bronwen	Hughes	US
burningfight	www.lomohomes.com/burningfight	Jens	Kaesemann	DE
cameraO	www.lomohomes.com/cameraO	Margarete	Eisele	DE
carmendevos	www.lomohomes.com/carmendevos	Carmen	De Vos	BE
c.c.w	www.lomohomes.com/c.c.w	Christina	Wittmann	DE
CentaurDean	www.lomohomes.com/CentaurDean	Dean	Chou	US
chuo104	www.lomohomes.com/chuo104	Dario	Alvarado	JP
clarissemerigeot0	www.lomohomes.com/clarissemerigeot0	Clarisse	Merigeot	FR
Cosmonaut	www.lomohomes.com/Cosmonaut	Mauricio	Arana Balcazar	CO
cynister	www.lomohomes.com/cynister	Cynthia	Eng-dinsel	US
czarone	www.lomohomes.com/czarone	Rene	Deckers	NL
dalbergaria	www.lomohomes.com/dalbergaria	Alexandre	d' Albergaria	US
damiao_santana	www.lomohomes.com/damiao_santana	Damião	Santana	BR
danuk	www.lomohomes.com/danuk	Daniel	Kaufmann	CH
dandan	www.lomohomes.com/dandan	Daniel	Liddington	GB
-DENVER-	www.lomohomes.com/-DENVER-	Denver	Leong	MY
domino	www.lomohomes.com/domino	John	Eldridge	GB
edita	www.lomohomes.com/edita	Edita	Knowler	AU
emay	www.lomohomes.com/EMay	Emily	May	GB
eraserhead	www.lomohomes.com/eraserhead	Greg	Limna	GB
faster1974	www.lomohomes.com/faster1974	Matthew	McConkey	GB
ferantoun	www.lomohomes.com/ferantoun	Fernanda	Antoun	BR
foundphotographer	www.lomohomes.com/foundphotographer	Adrian	Hanft	US
fphilippeaux	www.lomohomes.com/fphilippeaux	Franck	Philippeaux	FR
french_for_hi-hat	www.lomohomes.com/french_for_hi-hat	Matt	Walkerdine	GB
gagablabla	www.lomohomes.com/gagablabla	Narisa	Wattanasomsiri	TH
goldhammer	www.lomohomes.com/goldhammer	Jesper	Guldhammer	DK
goon	www.lomohomes.com/goon	Martin	Cattach	AU
gotreadgo	www.lomohomes.com/gotreadgo	Larry	Treadway	USA
gravityroom	www.lomohomes.com/gravityroom	Ted	Forbes	US

username	lomohome	first name	last name	country-iso
green_bananna	www.lomohomes.com/green_bananna	Anne	Kobayashi	CA
gumpwoy	www.lomohomes.com/gumpwoy	Mr.Kamol	Santaveemaneerat	TH
helmut_rec	www.lomohomes.com/helmut_rec	Mikko	Pitkänen	FI
hogwong	www.lomohomes.com/hogwong	David	Johnson	GB
holer	www.lomohomes.com/holer	Joel	Sotelo	US
Holgardo	www.lomohomes.com/Holgardo	Leonardo	Godnez Dávila	MX
holghino	www.lomohomes.com/holghino	Candido	Baldacchino	IT
iara_carvalho	www.lomohomes.com/iara_carvalho	Iara	Carvalho	BR
Ikhaan	www.lomohomes.com/Ikhaan	Nicolas	Quaegebeur	FR
isayhello	www.lomohomes.com/isayhello	Teerayut	Yukuntapornpong	TH
jazzgohan	www.lomohomes.com/jazzgohan	Stephane	Chabrier	FR
jbeninato	www.lomohomes.com/jbeninato	Jill	Beninato	US
jenv101	www.lomohomes.com/jenv101	Jennifer	Vandersteen	CA
jillog	www.lomohomes.com/jillog	Jillian	Pichocki	US
johnnyholga	www.lomohomes.com/johnnyholga	John	Allcot	GB
joncherry	www.lomohomes.com/joncherry	Jon	Cherry	GB
Jonee	www.lomohomes.com/Jonee	Jonathan	Worth	GB
jonheslop	www.lomohomes.com/jonheslop	Jon	Heslop	GB
josh1	www.lomohomes.com/josh1	Josh	Steinhaus	DE
karlbeck	www.lomohomes.com/karlbeck	Karl	Beck	US
kenzitaka	www.lomohomes.com/kenzitaka	Kenzi	Taka	MY
kitr	www.lomohomes.com/kitr	Christopher	Rosenberg	US
krebb	www.lomohomes.com/krebb	Kristy	Rebbeck	AU
kyng	www.lomohomes.com/kyng	Kachain	Bodinittidej	TH
littlecountrygirl	www.lomohomes.com/littlecountrygirl	Amanda	Voss	US
l_vagnozzi	www.lomohomes.com/l_vagnozzi	Luigi	Vagnozzi	IT
LOETZ	www.lomohomes.com/LOETZ	Branden	Loetz	US
londonhair	www.lomohomes.com/londonhair	Laura	Burlton	US
lovely_lena	www.lomohomes.com/lovely_lena	Lena	Källberg	SE
lurgee	www.lomohomes.com/lurgee	Lurgee	Lim	SG
madtwinsis	www.lomohomes.com/madtwinsis	Peggy	De Meue	BE
mandi	www.lomohomes.com/mandi	Mandi	Steininger	AT
Marcolitos	www.lomohomes.com/Marcolitos	Marco	Palumbo	GB
martinroe	www.lomohomes.com/martinroe	Martin	Roe	GB
melv	www.lomohomes.com/melv	Melvin	Gan	SG
michaelkuhle	www.lomohomes.com/michaelkuhle	Michael	Kuhle	US
mikerpaz	www.lomohomes.com/mikerpaz	Michele	Iannizzotto	IT
mikkelwurtz	www.lomohomes.com/mikkelwurtz	Mikkel	Würtz	DK
milchtrinken	www.lomohomes.com/milchtrinken	Friederike	Horn	DE
mimimalism	www.lomohomes.com/mimimalism	Mim	Stirling	AU
molotovcoketail	www.lomohomes.com/molotovcoketail	Dar Yang	Yan	MY
monta	www.lomohomes.com/monta	Marco	Montanari	IT
moominsean	www.lomohomes.com/moominsean	Sean	Rohde	US
Mosquitolo	www.lomohomes.com/Mosquitolo	Mirko	Nardecchia	IT
mtbbrian	www.lomohomes.com/mtbbrian	Brian	Schiele	US

username	lomohome	first name	last name	country-iso
naked	www.lomohomes.com/naked	Yao	Yichun	CN
neja	www.lomohomes.com/neja	Julia	Svetlova	RU
neve	www.lomohomes.com/neve	Bea	De giacomo	IT
Nina_ska	www.lomohomes.com/Nina_ska	Ninoska	Lamilla Olmedo	CL
nschaps	www.lomohomes.com/nschaps	Neil	Chapman	GB
okok	www.lomohomes.com/Okok	Arthur	Stachurski	US
OLDbEN	www.lomohomes.com/OLDbEN	Benjamin	Deering	AU
otto_blue	www.lomohomes.com/otto_blue	Scott	Feaster	US
OuroborosX	www.lomohomes.com/OuroborosX	Liad	Cohen	US
pandabear	www.lomohomes.com/pandabear	Mason	Dent	US
persona79	www.lomohomes.com/persona79	Jacob	Hawley	US
primeobjective	www.lomohomes.com/primeobjective	Chris	Keenan	GB
rebarbative	www.lomohomes.com/rebarbative	Teresa	Tavares	PT
rehnholm	www.lomohomes.com/rehnholm	Ulf	Rehnholm	SE
remitch	www.lomohomes.com/remitch	Rémi	Lavillonnière	FR
ringo_fyre	www.lomohomes.com/ringo_fyre	Martin	Doran	GB
ronin	www.lomohomes.com/ronin	Michael	Sailer	DE
san_san	www.lomohomes.com/san_san	Sandrine	Dedieu	FR
sandstep	www.lomohomes.com/sandstep	Ian	Kramar	US
saviorjosh	www.lomohomes.com/saviorjosh	Jianjun	Chen	CN
sbg1	www.lomohomes.com/sbg1	Shane	Goguen	US
scootiepye	www.lomohomes.com/scootiepye	Helen	Errington	GB
seanmichel	www.lomohomes.com/seanmichel	Sean	Duncan	US
self-taughtman	www.lomohomes.com/self-taughtman	Alekanikalia	Colipano	US
severin	www.lomohomes.com/severin	Severin	Matusek	AT
shadley25	www.lomohomes.com/shadley25	Sarah	Hadley	US
shadograf	www.lomohomes.com/shadograf	Tyler	D'Askquith	US
shanti929	www.lomohomes.com/shanti929	Shanti	Chang	TW
simplyironic	www.lomohomes.com/simplyironic	Jessica	Chia	SG
skac	www.lomohomes.com/skac	Stephanie	Kac	FR
SnapshotArtifact	www.lomohomes.com/SnapshotArtifact	James	Felder	US
SpacialK	www.lomohomes.com/SpacialK	Catherine	Rüttimann	CH
sqizo	www.lomohomes.com/sqizo	Ignasi	Perez	ES
tropi	www.lomohomes.com/tropi	Paolo	Di lucente	IT
ug3nia	www.lomohomes.com/ug3nia	Eugenia	Quiroga	AR
vaclavh	www.lomohomes.com/vaclavh	Vaclav	Hasek	US
valayres	www.lomohomes.com/valayres	Valentina	Ayres	BR
vincent.rose	www.lomohomes.com/vincent.rose	Vincent	Rose	US
Waind	www.lomohomes.com/Waind	Chris	Waind	NZ
weezerine	www.lomohomes.com/weezerine	Christine	Ko	AU
xbalboax	www.lomohomes.com/xbalboax	Demetri	Parides	US
xenin	www.lomohomes.com/xenin	Zora	Chan	MY
yammie	www.lomohomes.com/yammie	Yan Yan	Chan	HK

KODAK EBX

12   12A

ISBN: 3-902217-06-5

Printed in Hong Kong
First published in 2006 by the Lomographic Society International
Hollergasse 41, 1150 Vienna, Austria.
www.lomography.com

Front and back cover photographs by: Neil Chapman (nschaps)

Compiled by the Lomographic Society International and Adam Scott
Concept by Adam Scott (www.adamscottphotography.com)
Art Direction, Design & Illustration by Ninety (www.onedrinpen.com)
Edited by Lomographic Society International (www.lomography.com)
Coordinated by Severin Matusek

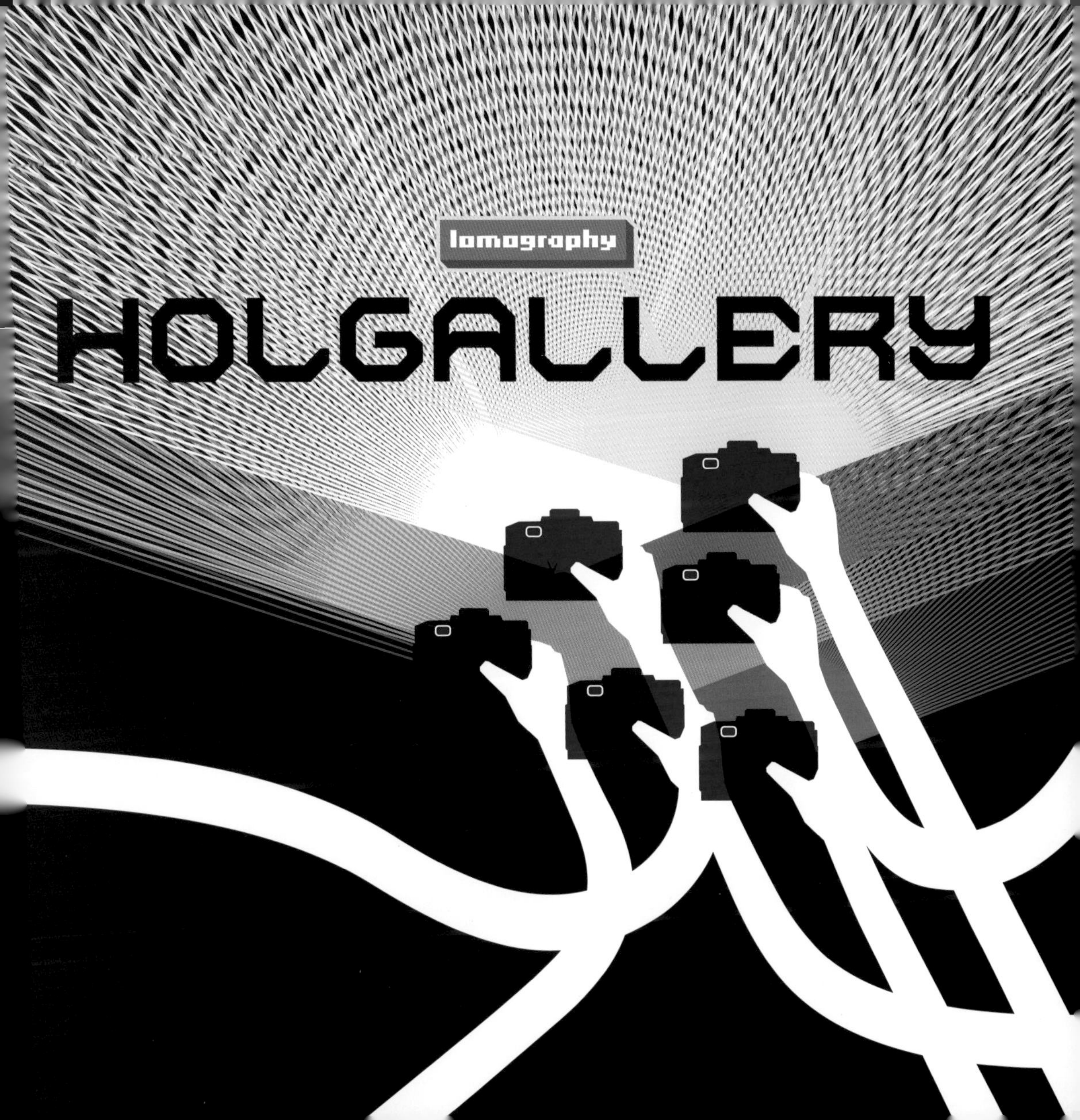
lomography
HOLGALLERY

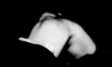

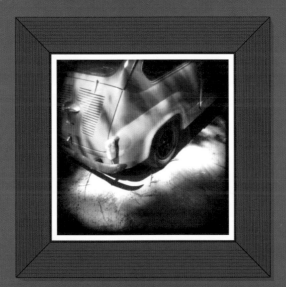

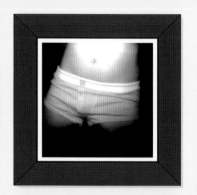

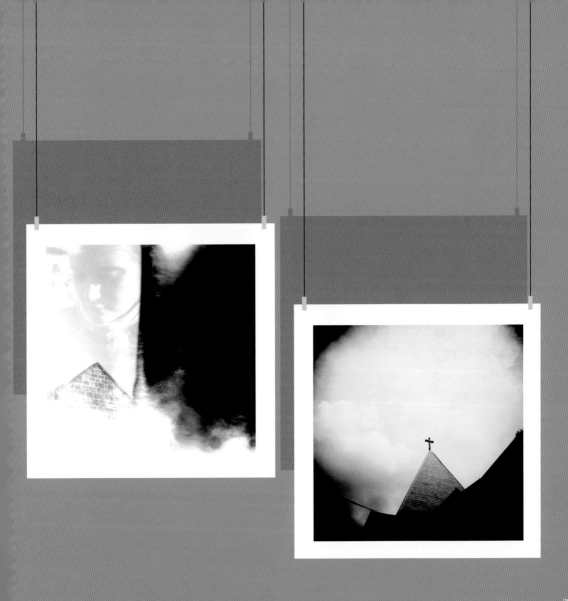

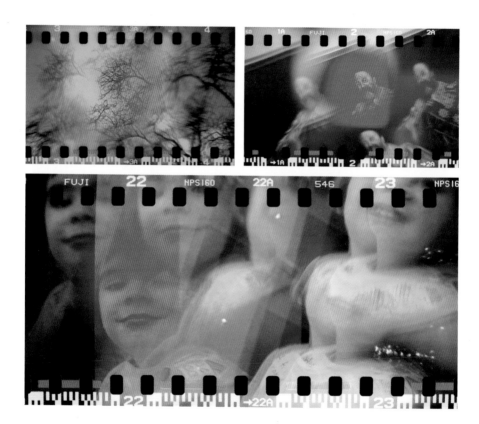

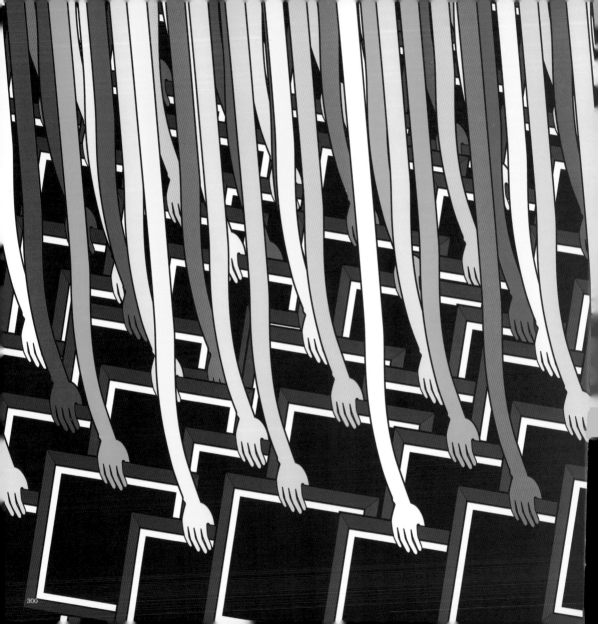

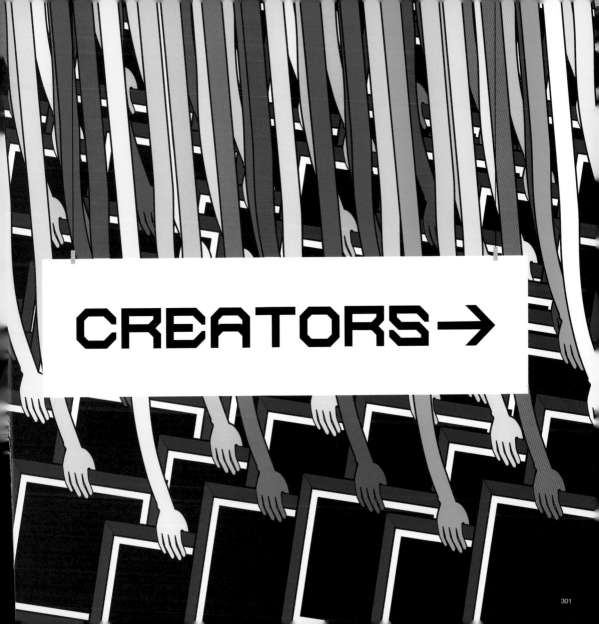

CREATORS→

CREATORS

Our full gratitude goes to the following Holga superstars for contributing their priceless work. The images are credited by page number, in order of appearance, reading from left to right and top to bottom, starting in the upper left corner.

HOLGALLERY
lomography

blackpot, blackpot, blackpot, blackpot, blackpot, blackpot
xenin
lurgee
akhsarual
jonee
Mickey Precious
jeansman, vincent.rose
londonhair
mosquitolo
saviourjosh
c.c.w, c.c.w
french_for_hi-hat, lurgee
goldhammer, goldhammer, goldhammer, SpacialK
littlecountrygirl, xevi, mikerpaz,
primeobjective
jillog
clarissemerigeot0
adamscott
otto_blue
cynister
londonhair
madtwinsis, jillog
shanti929
-DENVER-
holer
lovely_lena
jeansman
josh1
akhsarual
shanti929
gotreadgo, gotreadgo, gotreadgo, gotreadgo
mandi
clarissemerigeot0
clarissemerigeot0
jonheslop
jillog
londonhair
lurgee
007-0815-styler.de, OLDbEN
STRIP1: TiffanyWan, vaclavh, vaclavh.
STRIP2: otto_blue, OLDbEN
adamscott, adamscott, adamscott
lurgee, helmut_rec
Mauro
Marcolitos, OuroborosX
OuroborosX, Blackpot, akhsarual
OLDbEN, monta, martinroe, eraserhead
vaclavh, domino, hogwong, mandi, adamscott, french_for_hi-hat, jillog, krebb, browenhug,
bronwenhug, knottybenjamin, knottybenjamin, l_vagnozzi, l_vagnozzi, saru_, jonheslop
mandi, jillog, jonheslop, holer, neve, clarissemerigeot0, jazzgohan, jeansman, mtbbrian, jonheslop,
severin, clarissemerigeot0, sandstep, neja, shanti929, blackpot